1st Workshop on Computational Approaches to Compound Analysis

(ComAComA 2014)

Held at COLING 2014

Dublin, Ireland
24 August 2014

ISBN: 978-1-63439-225-9

Printed from e-media with permission by:

Curran Associates, Inc.
57 Morehouse Lane
Red Hook, NY 12571

Some format issues inherent in the e-media version may also appear in this print version.

Printed by Curran Associates, Inc. (2014)

For permission requests, please contact the Association for Computational Linguistics
at the address below.

Association for Computational Linguistics
209 N. Eighth Street
Stroudsburg, Pennsylvania 18360

Phone: 1-570-476-8006
Fax: 1-570-476-0860

acl@aclweb.org

Additional copies of this publication are available from:

Curran Associates, Inc.
57 Morehouse Lane
Red Hook, NY 12571 USA
Phone: 845-758-0400
Fax: 845-758-2634
Email: curran@proceedings.com
Web: www.proceedings.com

Introduction

The ComAComA workshop is an interdisciplinary platform for researchers working on compound processing in different languages, to present recent and ongoing work.

The workshop has several related aims. Firstly, it brings together researchers from different backgrounds (e.g., computational linguistics, linguistics, neurolinguistics, psycholinguistics, language technology) to discuss and evaluate compound processing each from their own point of view. Secondly, based on the interaction between the participants, the workshop provides an overview of existing and desired resources for future research in this area. Finally, we expect that the interdisciplinary approach of the workshop will result in better methodologies to evaluate compound processing systems from different perspectives.

Given the high productivity of compounding in a wide range of languages, compound processing is an interesting subject in linguistics, computational linguistics, and other applied disciplines. For example, for many language technology applications, compound processing remains a challenge (both morphologically and semantically), since novel compounds are created and interpreted on the fly. In order to deal with this productivity, systems that can analyse new compound forms and their meanings need to be developed. From an interdisciplinary perspective, we also need to better understand the process of compounding (as a cognitive process), in order to model its complexity.

Workshop Organizers

Ben Verhoeven, University of Antwerp, Belgium

Walter Daelemans, University of Antwerp, Belgium

Menno van Zaanen, Tilburg University, The Netherlands

Gerhard van Huyssteen, North-West University, South Africa

Program Committee

Preslav Nakov, Qatar Computing Research Institute

Iris Hendrickx, Radboud University Nijmegen

Lonneke Van der Plas, University of Stuttgart

Helmut Schmid, Ludwig Maximilian University Munich

Roald Eiselen, North-West University

Pavol Štekauer, P.J. Safarik University

Diarmuid Ó Séaghdha, University of Cambridge

Rochelle Lieber, University of New Hampshire

Tony Veale, University College Dublin

Pius ten Hacken, University of Innsbruck

Anneke Neijt, Radboud University Nijmegen

Andrea Krott, Univerisity of Birmingham

Emmanuel Keuleers, Ghent University

Stan Szpakowicz, University of Ottawa

Invited Speakers

Andrea Krott, University of Birmingham

Diarmuid Ó Séaghdha, University of Cambridge

Table of Contents

Modelling Regular Subcategorization Changes in German Particle Verbs

Stefan Bott **Sabine Schulte im Walde**
Institut für Maschinelle Sprachverabeitung
Universität Stuttgart
Pfaffenwaldring 5b, 70569 Stuttgart, Germany
{stefan.bott,schulte}@ims.uni-stuttgart.de

Abstract

German particle verbs are a type of multi word expression which is often compositional with respect to a base verb. If they are compositional they tend to express the same types of semantic arguments, but they do not necessarily express them in the same syntactic subcategorization frame: some arguments may be expressed by differing syntactic subcategorization slots and other arguments may be only implicit in either the base or the particle verb. In this paper we present a method which predicts syntactic slot correspondences between syntactic slots of base and particle verb pairs. We can show that this method can predict subcategorization slot correspondences with a fair degree of success.

1 Introduction

In German, particle verbs (PVs) are a very frequent and productive type of multi word expression. Particle verbs, such as *anstarren* (*to stare at*) in (1-a), are built from a base verb (BV) and a particle. Similar to other multi word expressions, German PVs may show a varying degree of compositionality with respect to the BV and to the particle. But German PVs also have another particularity: if they are compositional, the mapping from semantic arguments to syntactic subcategorization frames may be different between the PV and its corresponding BV.

(1) a. Die Katze starrt (den Vogel | die Wohnungstür) an.
The cat-N-nom stares (the bird-N-acc | the apartment_door-N-acc) at-PRT.
The cat stares at the (bird | apartment door).

b. Die Katze starrt auf den Vogel.
The cat-N-nom stares at-P the bird-acc.

c. Die Katze starrt zur Wohnungstür.
The cat-N-nom stares at-P the apartment_door-dat.

The events expressed with the PV *anstarren* in (1-a) can also be expressed with the BV *starren* in (1-b) and (1-c). But while the argument *Vogel* or *Wohnungstür* is expressed as an accusative object in (1-a) it is expressed as a PP in both (1-b) and (1-c), headed by the preposition *auf* and *zu*, respectively.

Related to this phenomenon, the change in the typical subcategorization frame from the BV to the PV can also lead to an incorporation or an addition of syntactic complements (Stiebels, 1996; Lüdeling, 2001), as illustrated by (2). The BV *bellen* (*to bark*) is strictly intransitive, while the corresponding PV *anbellen* (*to bark at*) is transitive and takes an obligatory accusative object which expresses the person or entity being barked at. This is a case of argument extensions in the PV with respect to its BV. The PV *anschrauben* (*to screw onto*) displays incorporation: it can nearly never select an argument which expresses the location onto which something is screwed, while its BV *schrauben* (*to screw*) requires the expression of the location with a PP.

Proceedings of the First Workshop on Computational Approaches to Compound Analysis, pages 1–10,
Dublin, Ireland, August 24 2014.

(2) a. Der Hund bellt.
The dog-N-nom barks.
b. Der Hund bellt den Postboten an.
The dog-N-nom barks the postman-N-acc at-PRT.
c. Der Mechaniker schraubt die Abdeckung auf die Öffnung.
The mechanic-N-nom screws the cover on the opening-N-acc.
d. Der Mechaniker schraubt die Abdeckung an.
The mechanic-N-nom screws the cover on-PRT.

(3) a. Der Metzger bringt seiner Frau Blumen.
The butcher brings his wife flowers.
The butcher brings his wife flowers.
b. Der Metzger bringt das Lämmchen um.
The butcher brings the little lamb PRT.
The butcher assassinates the little lamb.

Finally, if the meaning of the PV is not compositional with respect to the BV, there are no semantic correspondences between subcategorization slots of the PV and the BV. The problem of non-compositionality is illustrated by (3) which uses the PV *umbringen* (*to assassinate*), which has a totally different meaning from its BV *bringen* (*to bring*). A successful mapping between the subcategorization slots of both can thus be expected to have a direct relation to the assessment of PV compositionality.

The problem we address here can be called the *syntactic transfer problem*: the subcategorization frame of a BV can be mapped onto a subcategorization frame of the PV, where semantic arguments are not necessarily realized with the same syntactic positions in both of the verbs. A good approximation to this problem is potentially very useful in computational lexicography and other NLP tasks, such as machine translation and information extraction. We also expect it to be helpful to assess other aspects of German particle verbs, such as the prediction of compositionality levels.

In order to tackle the problem of argument slot matching we use a vector space model to represent distributional semantics. We expect that high distributional similarity between two given subcategorization slots taken from a verb pair signals a correspondence of these slots in a pair of subcategorization frames. On the contrary, we expect that low distributional similarity signals that no such correspondence can be established. Further on, if for a given subcategorization slot, either from a BV or a PV, no matching slot can be found in the complementary PV/BV automatically, this typically corresponds to a case of argument incorporation or argument extension.

In short, in this paper we make the following contributions: We present a method of automatically mapping syntactic subcategorization slots of BVs and PVs which is based on distributional semantics and we show that this method can outperform a random baseline with a high level of success.

The rest of this paper is organized as follows: In section 2 we present related work. Section 3 describes our experimental setup, including the method of correspondence prediction, the elicitation of human judgements and the evaluation. Section 4 presents the results which are then discussed in section 5. Section 6 concludes the paper with some final remarks and outlook on future work.

2 Related Work

Particle verbs have been studied from the theoretical perspective and, to a more limited extent, from the aspect of the computational identifiability, predictability of the degree of semantic compositionality (the transparency of their meaning with respect to the meaning of the base verb and the particle) and the semantic classifiabilty of PVs.

For English, there is work on the automatic extraction of PVs from corpora (Baldwin and Villavicencio, 2002; Baldwin, 2005; Villavicencio, 2005) and the determination of compositionality (McCarthy et al., 2003; Baldwin et al., 2003; Bannard, 2005). To the best of our knowledge Aldinger (2004) is the first work that studies German PVs from a corpus based perspective, with an emphasis on the syntactic behavior and syntactic change. Schulte im Walde (2004; 2005; 2006) presents several preliminary distributional studies to explore salient features at the syntax-semantics interface that determine the semantic nearest neighbours of German PVs. Relying on the insights of those studies, Schulte im Walde (2006) and Hartmann (2008) present preliminary experiments on modelling the subcategorization transfer of German PVs with respect to their BVs, in order to strengthen PV-BV distributional similarity. The main goal for them is to use transfer information in order to predict the degree of semantic compositionality of PVs. Kühner and Schulte im Walde (2010) use unsupervised clustering to determine the degree of compositionality of German PVs, via common PV-BV cluster membership. They are, again, mainly interested in the assessment of compositionality, which is done on the basis of lexical information. They use syntactic information, but only as a filter and for lexical heads as cooccurrence features in order to limit the selected argument slots to certain syntactic functions. They compare different feature configurations and conclude that the best results can be obtained with information stemming from direct objects and PP-objects. The incorporation of syntactic information in the form of dependency arc labels (concatenated with the head nouns) does not yield satisfactory results, putting the syntactic transfer problem in evidence, the problem which we address here. They conclude that an incorporation of syntactic transfer information between BVs and PVs could possibly improve the results. In Bott and Schulte im Walde (2014a) we present a method to assess PV compositionality without recurring to any syntactic features, but we assume that the results of this method could be improved if additional syntactic transfer information was incorporated.

Based on a theoretical study (Springorum, 2011) which explains particle meanings in terms of Discourse Representation Theory (Kamp and Reyle, 1993), Springorum et al. (2012) show that four classes of PVs with the particle *an* can be classified automatically. They take a supervised approach using decision trees. The use of decision trees also allows them to manually inspect and analyze the decisions made by the classifier. As predictive features they use the head nouns of objects, generalized classes of these nouns and PP types. In Bott and Schulte im Walde (2014b) we present an experiment to classify semantic classes of PVs, based on subcategorization information stemming from both the BV and the BV of each BV-PV pair. In this work we use the same gold standard we use here. This experiment is also related to the one presented here in that we assume that the syntactic transfer patterns are quite stable within semantic classes.

3 Experimental Setup

In order to test our hypothesis we selected a set of 32 PVs listed in Fleischer and Barz (2012), including 14 PVs with the particle *an* and 18 with the particle *auf*.[1] We concentrated on two particles here in order to have a small and controlled test bed which allows us to study the syntactic transfers. We selected verbs which we considered to be highly compositional in order to be able to study the correspondence of subcategorization slots. The set contained verbs which have argument slots which are typically realized as different syntactic subcategorizations. The set also contained PVs which show argument incorporation or the introduction of an additional syntactic complement with respect to their BV. We excluded verbs which we could clearly perceive as being polysemous. This set of verbs was processed automatically and presented to human raters, as described below. The test set can be seen in table 1. This test set was already used in Bott and Schulte im Walde (2014b), where it was used as a gold standard for the automatic classification of semantic classes of particle verbs, based on syntactic transfer patterns. The subcategorization patterns listed here are the ones we *expected* to find, so the second and the third row together represent the expected syntactic transfer pattern. The values given in these two columns are a lexicographic presentation of the transfer patterns we expected to find. The task of the system was defined as to find matches between slots from both verbs automatically. The verbs were grouped together in classes which are both semantically similar and also expected to have a similar syntactic behaviour. The labels in the column for the *semantic class* are taken from Fleischer and Barz (2012), but broken down into more detailed classes, such as verbs of *trying*, *gaze* or *sound*. The latter label extensions were

[1]Fleischer and Barz list more than 100 PVs for both *an* and *auf*, but they embed this listing in a descriptive text. Some of the verbs listed are very rare or highly ambiguous. Since particle verbs in German are a highly productive paradigm and give rise to many neologisms, compiling a complete list of PVs is nearly impossible.

added by us. In the present work we are not interested in the semantic classes as such, but we assume that the transfer patterns are similar in each semantic class.

3.1 Automatic Classification

Since we wanted to test the predictability of syntactic slot correspondences, we first had to identify the typical elements of the subcategorization frames for both BVs and PVs. In order to do so, we extracted all observable subcategorization patterns from a parsed corpus. Then we selected the 5 most frequent subcategorization patterns for each verb (either BV or PV). These patterns were then broken down into their individual elements. The simple transitive pattern, for example, contained a subject and an accusative object. Since some subordinate structures miss overt subjects and in German all verbs have a subject slot, we always included the subject in the representation of all verbs. The rationale behind this method, which is based on the frequency of subcategorization patterns rather than the frequency of slots, was that we were not interested in subcategorization slots *per se*, but in subcategorization patterns as a typical representation structure in computational lexicography.

Then we built a vector space model for all possible combinations of BV-complements and PV-complements of each BV-PV pair. The dimensions of the vector were instantiated by the head nouns of the syntactic relation in question. The extension in each dimension is equal to the frequency of the head noun in the relevant position. For this experiment no term weighting was applied. Table 2 shows the strongest dimensions for the vectors corresponding to the PP-argument headed by the verbs *heften* (*to attach*) and *anheften* (*to attach to*). The two verbs can be used in quite similar contexts with very similar arguments. Accordingly, the two vectors are similar to each other. Although the two vectors correspond to PP slots headed by the preposition *an*, it can be seen that there is a syntactic transfer from accusative to dative case. Both vectors include head nouns expressing typical places to which things can be attached to, such as a *pin board* (*Pinnwand*), a *wall* (*Wand*) or a *board* (*Brett*). The verb *heften* is frequently found in the idiom *sich an jemandes Ferse heften* (*to attach onseself to someone's heels*, which means *to follow someone closely*), while this idiom cannot be formed with the PV *anheften*. For this reason the dimension for *Ferse* is very strong. This example, especially the vector for *anheften* also shows that the features are often sparsely represented, which presents a problem for our approach.

As a similarity measure we used the cosine distance between two vectors. A variable threshold was applied on the cosine distance to, which serves to separate corresponding subcategorization slots from non-corresponding ones. This is especially important for the detection of argument incorporation or argument extension (cf. example (2)). If, for example, for a given BV slot no PV slot can be found with a cosine value above the threshold, we interpret this as a case of argument extension. On the other hand, a slot from a PV which cannot be match to a slot of its BV is taken to signal argument incorporation. Among the vectors compared to each target subcategorization slot only the one with the highest cosine value was considered as a possible correspondence. Finally, since we want to capture both argument incorporation and argument extension, we computed correspondences for both BVs and PVs separately. Even if this means that most slot pairs are computed twice, this allowed zero-correspondences for slots from both verbs. It theoretically also allows for one-to-many and many-to-one matches, even if we did not exploit them here. We excluded closed class dependencies of verbs, such as negations. We also excluded clausal complements, because they could not be properly represented by our vector extraction method. To get an idea of the lower bound of the outcome values, we used a select-1 baseline. This baseline was obtained by calculating the expected precision and recall for the case that for each subcategorization slot a matching slot from the corresponding other verb is assigned randomly.

As training data we used a lemmatized and tagged version of the SDeWaC corpus (Faaß and Eckart, 2013), a corpus of nearly 885 million words. The corpus was processed with the Mate dependency parser (Bohnet, 2010). The output of this parser represents the syntactic complements of the verbs as labelled arcs. In the case of nominal objects the nominal heads could be directly read of the dependent nodes and the syntactic relation of the arc labels. In the case of PP-complements we read the nominal heads of the nominal node which depends on the preposition which in turn depends on the verb. For the extraction of features we could rely on the database compiled by (Scheible et al., 2013).

Particle	Typical frames for the BV	Typical frames for the PV	Semantic Class	Verbs in Class	
an	NPnom +NPacc +PP-an	NPnom +NPacc +PP-an	locative/ relational tying	an|binden an|ketten	to tie at to chain at
	NPnom +PP-zu/in/ nach/auf	NPnom +NPacc	locative/ relational gaze	an|blicken an|gucken an|starren	to glance at to look at to stare at
	NPnom +NPacc +PP-mit	NPnom +NPacc +PP-mit	ingressive consump- tion	an|brechen an|reißen an|schneiden	start to break start to tear start to cut
	NPnom	NPnom +NPacc	locative/ relational sound	an|brüllen an|fauchen an|meckern	to roar at to hiss at to bleat at
	NPnom +NPacc +PP-an	NPnom +NPacc	locative/ relational fixation	an|heften an|kleben an|schrauben	to stick at to glue at to screw at
auf	NPnom	NPnom	locative blaze- bubble	auf|brodeln auf|flammen auf|lodern auf|spudeln	to bubble up to light up to blaze up to bubble up
	NPnom +PP-zu/in/ nach/auf	NPnom	locative gaze	auf|blicken auf|schauen auf|sehen	to glance up to look up to look up
	NPnom +NPacc	NPnom +NPacc	locative/ dimensional instigate	auf|hetzen auf|scheuchen	to instigate to rouse
	NPnom +NPacc +PP-auf	NPnom +NPacc	locative/ relational fixation	auf|heften auf|kleben auf|pressen	to staple on to glue on to press on
	NPnom	NPnom	ingressive sound	auf|brüllen auf|heulen auf|klingen auf|kreischen auf|schluchzen auf|stöhnen	suddenly roar suddenly howl suddenly sound suddenly scream suddenly sob suddenly moan

Table 1: The gold standard classes for the experiments, with subcategorization patterns.

anheften-MO-an-dat	count	**heften-MO-an-acc**	count
Oberfläche	3	Ferse	154
Gerichtstafel	3	Brust	48
Stelle	2	Revers	43
Schluss	2	Kreuz	32
Unterlage	1	Wand	30
Kirchentüre	1	Spur	12
Brett	1	Tafel	11
Pinnwand	1	Fahne	11
Körper	1	Tür	11
Wand	1	Pinnwand	9
Bauchdecke	1	Kleid	6
Baum	1	Brett	6
Schleimhautzelle	1	Mastbaum	6
Himmel	1	Körper	5
Spur	1	ihn	5
Sphäre	1	Kleidung	5
Wand	1	Oberfläche	5
Spur	1	Stelle	4
Engstelle	1	Baum	4
Pflanze	1	Jacke	4
Protein	1	Mantel	4
Unterseite	1	Teil	3
Zweig	1	Krebszelle	3
Pin-Wand	1	schwarz	3

Table 2: The strongest dimensions for two sample vectors representing subcategorization slots of the verbs *heften* and *anheften*.

3.2 Human rating elicitation

We asked human raters to rate the same examples which the system classified automatically. Each of the pairs of subcategorization slots described in section 3.1 was rated individually. The pairs were always presented in the order <BV-subcategorization-slot,PV-subcategorization-slot> and in visual blocks corresponding to BV subcategorization slots. So the raters could see the possible PV subcategorization slots in direct comparison. The order of blocks was randomized. The raters were asked to judge every pair and rate whether or not they could correspond to a single semantic argument. They were invited to invent example sentences, but because of the length of the annotation session they were not asked to write them down. They were told that, as a criterion for semantic correspondence, each of the verbs in a pair should be usable to describe at least one event or situation they could think of. One annotation example, which did not stem from the set to be rated, was given.

Four human raters were asked to rate examples. All annotators were experts with either a linguistic or NLP background. They were all German native speakers and none of them was otherwise involved in the work presented in this paper. Because of the large size of the data set to be annotated we had to distribute the set over two annotation forms and each annotation form was annotated by two raters. Before the annotation started, one of the authors carried out the same annotation in order to estimate the time needed for each annotation and the level of success which could be expected from the system. Also this annotation was done blindly, without knowledge of the system output, but with a precise knowledge of the task.

The annotation turned out to be much more difficult that we had originally expected. The annotators described the annotation as being hard to perform. This was also reflected by inter annotator agreement; we could only observe a fair agreement, with a Fleiss' Kappa score of 0.31. The agreement between the annotator ratings and the rating by the author was somewhat higher with a Fleiss' Kappa score of 0.44. Some annotators gave detailed feedback, once they had completed the annotation.

4 Results

Table 3 shows the results we obtained. The columns show precision, recall and the harmonic F-score obtained by comparing the system output to the human ratings. We used a precision/recall schema because the task can be seen as the system selecting the most likely slot correspondences from a set of all possible correspondences. So a true positive is obtained if the system selects the same slot that a human rater would select. False positives correspond to a slot selected by the system, which was not chosen by the annotator and a false negative instances are those which are marked by an annotator and not chosen by the system.[2] Since there was more than one annotators and the annotations differed, we took the sum of true and falls positives and false negatives from all annotators and calculated the scores over this sum. The last column shows the harmonic F-score values we obtained with the annotations produced by one of the authors. The lines represent those threshold values for which the highest precision or F-score could be obtained. The last line represents the baseline. Since a variable threshold was applied there is a trade-off between precision and recall. This is represented in figure 1, which displays the same information as table 3, but in a graphical way.

As expected, the precision improves with higher thresholds, but this comes at the cost of a lower recall. The F-score stays relatively constant. The baseline is quite low, especially the recall. This can be explained because the human raters were free to assign zero-correspondences (i.e. argument incorporations or argument extensions, as exemplified by the examples in (2)) or more than one correspondence per target slot.

5 Discussion

We could observe that the system can predict the correspondences between syntactic subcategorization slots to a fair degree of success and that our method can clearly outperform the baseline. Our hypotheses

[2]Precision was calculated as $\frac{\{true\ positives\}}{\{true\ positives\}+\{false\ positives\}}$ and recall as $\frac{\{true\ positives\}}{\{true\ positives\}+\{false\ negatives\}}$. The F-score was calculated as $(precision + recall)/2$.

Threshold	Precision	Recall	F-score	Author F-score
0.15	0.48	0.38	0.43	**0.68**
0.6	0.69	0.21	**0.45**	0.63
0.85	**0.75**	0.14	0.44	0.59
baseline	0.38	0.23	0.31	0.31

Table 3: Results of the evaluation in precision, recall and harmonic F-score. The last column represents the pilot annotation carried out by one of the authors.

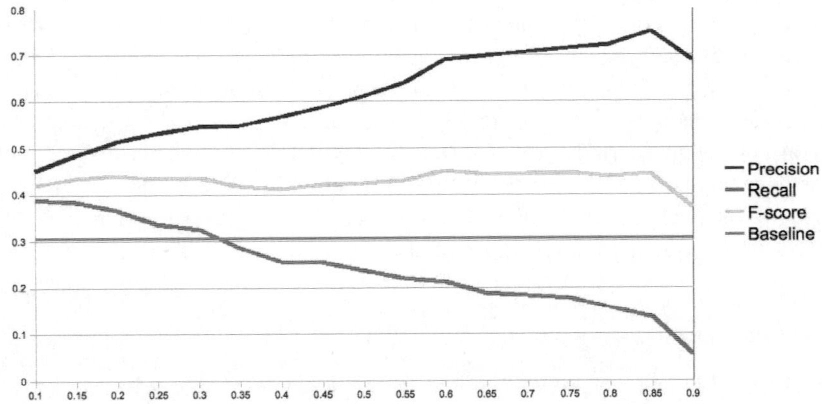

Figure 1: Trade-off between precision and recall. The F-Score remains relatively stable.

that correspondence between subcategorization slots can be predicted to a large degree by distributional semantic similarity can thus be confirmed. On the other hand, the success was not as high as we initially expected. It is surprising that the precision and recall values obtained with the annotations of the human raters are much lower than the values obtained in the initial annotation produced by the author. The author annotation has to be seen as overly optimistic, since it was done with a deeper understanding of the computational task which was to be carried out by the system. Still, this annotation was done blindly. So the big difference we observed is surprising. As already mentioned, the annotators all reported that they found the annotation task difficult to carry out and we attribute the low agreement to this difficulty. The fact that the agreement among different rather was also only fair ($\kappa = 0.31$) hints in the same direction. It must be said that some annotators found the annotation task more difficult than others. Two of the raters reported less annotation difficulty than the remaining. These two annotators were also the ones with most annotation experience and they were both familiar with the topic of particle verbs from a theoretical perspective. When the system output was compared to the ratings of best annotator, a maximum F-score of 0.55 could be achieved, which is still lower than the values obtained in comparison to the author annotation, but much higher than the average of all annotations.

Since some of the annotators gave detailed comments after the annotation was completed, we could detect some problems, which made the annotation difficult, but also extends to the automatic matching. For example, some base verbs have a resultative reading which do not express an *agent* and match the *patient* with the nominal subject position. One such verb is *kleben* (*to stick/glue*) as exemplified in (4). Accordingly among the strongest dimensions of the vector that represents the subject slot of *kleben*, many nouns appear, which are typical things that stick, such as *band aids* (*Pflaster*), *dough* (*Teig*) and *blood* (*Blut*). The closest vector to the vector for the accusative object vector of *ankleben* was also the accusative object vector of *kleben* (cosine=0.64), but the subject vector was still relatively strong (cosine=0.19).

(4) a. Gerda klebt den Zettel an die Tür.
Gerda sticks the Note on the door.
b. Der Zettel klebt an der Tür.
The Note sticks-to the door.

The particle verb *ankleben* can be used to describe the same state of affairs as in (4-a), but not as in (4-b). This is evidently a problem which is hard to solve with our approach because the correspondence of slots from BV and PV interferes with a slot correspondence among different uses of the BV.[3]

Finally, we found that many of the feature vectors were sparsely instantiated. This can be seen, for example, in the vector that represents the dative PP modifier headed by *an* of the verb *anheften* shown in table 2. The sparsity problem could be remedied by reducing the number of dimensions with the application of some kind of abstraction over the head nouns. For example the concepts of *Tür* (*door*) and *Kirchentür* (*church door*) are strongly related and could be represented in one dimension of the feature vector. The same holds for the concepts of *Pinnwand* (*pin board*), *Wand* (*wall*) and *Tafel* (*blackboard*) and other groups of concepts. With a certain level of abstraction over such concepts, the distance between vectors would also be reduced in case they are sparse. This abstraction is, however, not a trivial problem in itself. The application of lexical ontologies like WordNet (as used by e.g. Springorum et al. (2012)), for example, has the danger of reducing the semantics of head nouns to level of abstraction which is too high, since WordNet has only few top-level categories and few levels of conceptual inheritance.

6 Conclusion and Outlook

We started the work described in this paper out of an interest to approach the syntactic transfer problem of German particle verbs from a computational perspective. We wanted to know in how far the subcategorization slots of a particle verb can be associated with subcategorization slots of a base verbs from which it is derived. The information we used for this matching is based on distributional semantics. We could show that can be done with a good degree of success. From the elicitation of human judgements we learned that the task is also not an easy one for human raters. This also sheds some light on the difficulty of the problem as a computational task.

The work we present here is relevant for computational lexicography. Firstly it can help relate lexical entries of such closely related lexical items as particle verbs and the base verbs they incorporate. The findings we made here may be also applicable to other types of multi word expressions.

In future work we would like to remedy the problem sparse vector representation with the use of abstraction over the head-nouns which will reduce the dimensionality of the feature vector. We also plan to see in how far an automatic clustering of particle verbs into semantic groups can strengthen the prediction of slot correspondences under the assumption that semantically similar verbs tend to undergo the same syntactic transfer. Finally, the problem of syntactic transfer between two elements is also related to the predictability of the degree of compositionality between BV-PV pairs. We are especially interested in this last problem and in future work we plan to investigate in which way subcategorization slot matching can be used as a predictor for compositionality levels.

Acknowledgements

This work was funded by the DFG Research Project "Distributional Approaches to Semantic Relatedness" (Stefan Bott, Sabine Schulte im Walde), and the DFG Heisenberg Fellowship SCHU-2580/1-1 (Sabine Schulte im Walde). We would also like to thank the participants of the human rating experiment.

References

Nadine Aldinger. 2004. Towards a Dynamic Lexicon: Predicting the Syntactic Argument Structure of Complex Verbs. In *Proceedings of the 4th International Conference on Language Resources and Evaluation*, Lisbon, Portugal.

[3]This problem is similar to the prediction of argument realizations in diathesis alternations, such as pairs found in pairs of sentences like "The boy rolled the ball down the hill" vs "the ball rolled down the hill".

Timothy Baldwin and Aline Villavicencio. 2002. Extracting the Unextractable: A Case Study on Verb Particles. In *Proceedings of the Sixth Conference on Computational Natural Language Learning*, pages 98–104, Taipei, Taiwan.

Timothy Baldwin, Colin Bannard, Takaaki Tanaka, and Dominic Widdows. 2003. An Empirical Model of Multiword Expression Decomposability. In *Proceedings of the ACL-2003 Workshop on Multiword Expressions: Analysis, Acquisition and Treatment*, pages 89–96, Sapporo, Japan.

Timothy Baldwin. 2005. Deep Lexical Acquisition of Verb–Particle Constructions. *Computer Speech and Language*, 19:398–414.

Collin Bannard. 2005. Learning about the Meaning of Verb–Particle Constructions from Corpora. *Computer Speech and Language*, 19:467–478.

Bernd Bohnet. 2010. Top Accuracy and Fast Dependency Parsing is not a Contradiction. In *Proceedings of the 23rd International Conference on Computational Linguistics*, pages 89–97, Beijing, China.

Stefan Bott and Sabine Schulte im Walde. 2014a. Optimizing a Distributional Semantic Model for the Prediction of German Particle Verb Compositionality. In *Proceedings of the 9th International Conference on Language Resources and Evaluation*, pages 509–516, Reykjavik, Iceland.

Stefan Bott and Sabine Schulte im Walde. 2014b. Syntactic Transfer Patterns of German Particle Verbs and their Impact on Lexical Semantics. In *Proceedings of the Third Joint Conference on Lexical and Computational Semantics*, Dublin, Ireland.

Gertrud Faaß and Kerstin Eckart. 2013. SdeWaC – a Corpus of Parsable Sentences from the Web. In *Proceedings of the International Conference of the German Society for Computational Linguistics and Language Technology*, Darmstadt, Germany.

Wolfgang Fleischer and Irmhild Barz. 2012. *Wortbildung der deutschen Gegenwartssprache*. Walter de Gruyter, 4th edition.

Silvana Hartmann. 2008. Einfluss syntaktischer und semantischer Subkategorisierung auf die Kompositionalität von Partikelverben. Studienarbeit. Institut für Maschinelle Sprachverarbeitung, Universität Stuttgart. Supervision: Sabine Schulte im Walde and Hans Kamp.

Hans Kamp and Uwe Reyle. 1993. *From discourse to logic: Introduction to modeltheoretic semantics of natural language, formal logic and discourse representation theory*. Number 42. Springer.

Natalie Kühner and Sabine Schulte im Walde. 2010. Determining the Degree of Compositionality of German Particle Verbs by Clustering Approaches. In *Proceedings of the 10th Conference on Natural Language Processing*, pages 47–56, Saarbrücken, Germany.

Anke Lüdeling. 2001. *On German Particle Verbs and Similar Constructions in German*. Dissertations in Linguistics. CSLI Publications, Stanford, CA.

Diana McCarthy, Bill Keller, and John Carroll. 2003. Detecting a Continuum of Compositionality in Phrasal Verbs. In *Proceedings of the ACL-SIGLEX Workshop on Multiword Expressions: Analysis, Acquisition and Treatment*, Sapporo, Japan.

Silke Scheible, Sabine Schulte im Walde, Marion Weller, and Max Kisselew. 2013. A Compact but Linguistically Detailed Database for German Verb Subcategorisation relying on Dependency Parses from a Web Corpus: Tool, Guidelines and Resource. In *Proceedings of the 8th Web as Corpus Workshop*, pages 63–72, Lancaster, UK.

Sabine Schulte im Walde. 2004. Identification, Quantitative Description, and Preliminary Distributional Analysis of German Particle Verbs. In *Proceedings of the COLING Workshop on Enhancing and Using Electronic Dictionaries*, pages 85–88, Geneva, Switzerland.

Sabine Schulte im Walde. 2005. Exploring Features to Identify Semantic Nearest Neighbours: A Case Study on German Particle Verbs. In *Proceedings of the International Conference on Recent Advances in Natural Language Processing*, pages 608–614, Borovets, Bulgaria.

Sabine Schulte im Walde. 2006. The Syntax-Semantics Interface of German Particle Verbs. Panel discussion at the 3rd ACL-SIGSEM Workshop on Prepositions at the 11th Conference of the European Chapter of the Association for Computational Linguistics.

Sylvia Springorum, Sabine Schulte im Walde, and Antje Roßdeutscher. 2012. Automatic Classification of German *an* Particle Verbs. In *Proceedings of the 8th International Conference on Language Resources and Evaluation*, pages 73–80, Istanbul, Turkey.

Sylvia Springorum. 2011. DRT-based Analysis of the German Verb Particle *"an"*. *Leuvense Bijdragen*, 97:80–105.

Barbara Stiebels. 1996. *Lexikalische Argumente und Adjunkte. Zum semantischen Beitrag von verbalen Präfixen und Partikeln*. Akademie Verlag, Berlin.

Aline Villavicencio. 2005. The Availability of Verb-Particle Constructions in Lexical Resources: How much is enough? *Computer Speech & Language*, 19(4):415–432.

Splitting of Compound Terms in non-Prototypical Compounding Languages

Elizaveta Clouet and **Béatrice Daille**
LINA, University of Nantes
{elizaveta.clouet,beatrice.daille}@univ-nantes.fr

Abstract

Compounding is present in a large variety of languages in different proportions. Compound rate in the text obviously depends on the language, but also on the genre and the domain. Scientific and technical texts are especially conducive to compounding, even in the languages that are not traditionally admitted as highly compounding ones. In this article we address compound splitting of specialized terms. We propose a multi-lingual method of compound recognition and splitting, which uses corpus frequencies, lexical data and optionally linguistic rules. This is a supervised method which requires a small amount of segmented compounds as input. We evaluate the method on two languages that rarely serve as a material for automatic splitting systems: English and Russian. The results obtained are competitive with those of a state-of-the-art corpus-driven approach.

1 Introduction

Compounding is a method of word formation consisting of a combination of two (or more) lexical elements that form a unit of meaning. In this work we only handle so called "closed compounds" (Macherey et al., 2011), i.e. those forming also a graphical unit. A great number of languages resort to this word formation. In some of them such as German, Dutch (Germanic family), Estonian or Finnish (Uralic family) compounding is very regular and well described. In other languages it is less productive (e.g. Slavic family), or even marginal (most of Romance languages). This phenomenon is particularly productive in specialized domains because of the necessity to denote the domain concepts in a very concise and precise way. In addition, specialized texts contain many neoclassical compounds (Namer, 2009), i.e. compounds with some elements of Greek or Latin etymological origin: *hydro* + *logy* = *hydrology*.

In this article we discuss processing of compound terms, and we carry out the experiments with English and Russian, which are not prototypical compounding languages. As a matter of fact, compounding in English is rather productive and widely investigated in linguistic studies. But this language is rarely subject to experiments in automatic compound splitting. The first reason is that most of English compounds are formed by simple concatenation (*airfoil* = *air* + *foil*, *streamtube* = *stream* + *tube*), so their splitting is supposed to be straightforward. The second reason is that many compounds in highly compounding languages should be translated into English as multi-word expressions. That is why the works addressing automatic compound splitting in the context of machine translation often admit that English contains only few closed compounds (Koehn and Knight, 2003; Macherey et al., 2011). In these works, the use of English parallel texts helps to extract the multi-word equivalents of compounds from the texts in highly compounding languages. We assume that English compound terms are still worth splitting and analyzing. The first reason is that the assumption of independent occurring of English compound elements fails when we consider neoclassical compounds. The second ground is that distinguishing between compounds and non-compound out-of-dictionary words (named entities, derivative forms, etc.) can be problematic.

Proceedings of the First Workshop on Computational Approaches to Compound Analysis, pages 11–19,
Dublin, Ireland, August 24 2014.

In the Russian language the elements of compounds do not often appear as independent words in texts, for example:

водоснабжение 'water supply'
vodosnabzhenie[1] = voda 'water' + snabzhenie 'supply'

Here the inflection "a" of the first component is omitted and the linking morpheme "o" is inserted.

Compounding in Russian is less regular than, for instance, in German. Therefore most of NLP systems for Russian, to our knowledge, store usual compound parts in the lexicon. For specialized vocabularies this solution does not seem to be sufficient, since the new compounds terms constantly appear.

To handle compounds in typologically different languages, including languages with non-independent components, we propose a corpus-driven splitting system using also string similarity and able to integrate language-specific rules[2].

The article has the following structure. Section 2 gives a review of some compound splitting methods proposed in the literature. Section 3 presents our splitting method. In Section 4 the experiments and data are described. We discuss the results and analyse the errors. We also compare our system to the state-of-the-art corpus-based method of Koehn and Knight (2003). We conclude with Section 5.

2 Related Works

Compound splitting was addressed in many NLP works, as a standalone task or in the pipeline of another application: machine translation (Koehn and Knight, 2003; Macherey et al., 2011; Stymne et al., 2013), information retrieval (Braschler and Ripplinger, 2004; Chen and Gey, 2001), etc.

To deal with the non-independent compound elements in morphologically rich languages, different solutions have been proposed. It is possible to store separately the compound stems and the linking morphemes (the morphemes that are inserted at the component boundaries to form a compound), and to have a grammar to combine them. This solution is realized in the morphological analyser for German SMOR (Schmid et al., 2004). The construction of such a finite-state morphology for a new language is a costly task in terms of time and efforts.

Another approach is to formalize the component modifications as a set of rules describing addition, but also deletion and substitution of some character sequences on the component boundaries within a compound. Thus, the compound splitter BananaSplit (Ott, 2005) uses a set of linguistic rules for German to restore independent forms from compound forms, and validates the restored forms with the help of a monolingual dictionary.

Other methods resort to the corpora to validate the analyses. A pioneering work using corpus statistics for compound splitting was done by Koehn and Knight (2003). The algorithm generates all possible segmentations for a given word (taking into account some linking morphemes), and gives a probability for each segmentation, estimated from the geometric mean of the component frequencies in the corpus. The segmentation with the highest score is classed as the best.

Probabilistic splitting methods using machine learning technologies have been proposed (Dyer, 2009; Hewlett and Cohen, 2011; Macherey et al., 2011). Actually they are less precise than the language-specific methods, but their advantage is the usability for any language. Statistical methods also tend to integrate some linguistic knowledge (e.g. list of linking morphemes).

3 Compound Splitting Method

Our concern was to design a corpus-driven system that could be applied to different languages, but also able to integrate linguistic knowledge. For a given word, the system makes the decision as to whether it is a compound, and for compounds it gives one or several candidate analyses ranked by their scores (in this work we use up to five candidates). Figure 1 illustrates the splitting mechanism, as well as the system training needed to set up splitting parameters.

[1]Here and further for Russian examples transliteration is given.

[2]https://logiciels.lina.univ-nantes.fr/redmine/projects/compost

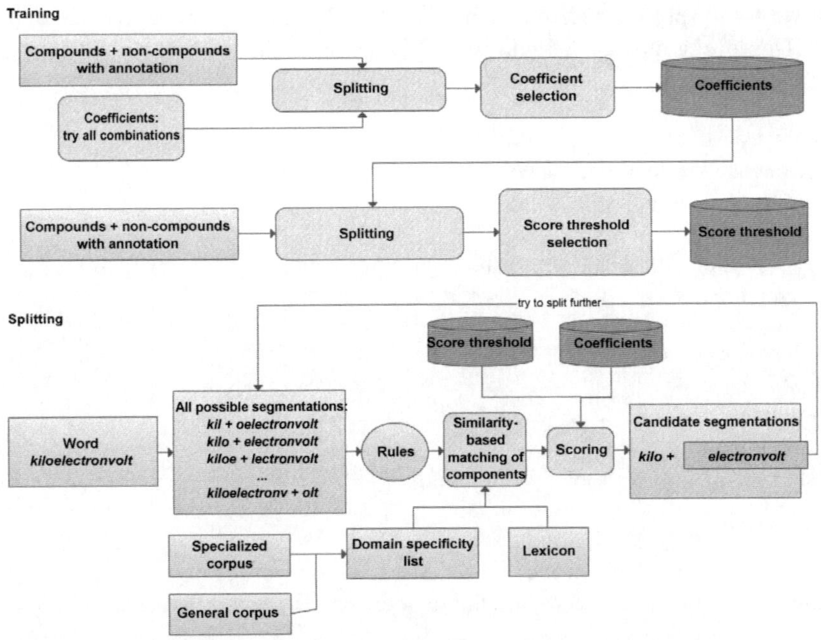

Figure 1: Parameters setting and compound splitting

3.1 General Method Description

To split a candidate compound, we start generating all its possible two-part segmentations beginning with the components of minimum permitted length: we used the minimum length of 3 characters, which is a frequent choice for compound splitting systems (Koehn and Knight, 2003; Dyer, 2009).

RU ветротурбина 'wind turbine'
vetroturbina → vet + roturbina
vetroturbina → vetr + oturbina
vetroturbina → vetro + turbina
...
vetroturbina → vetroturb + ina

If we can provide rules for this language to restore independent lexemes from non-independent components, we apply them to the component candidates. We will further refer to these rules as "linguistic rules" or simply "rules". For English only a few rules for correcting lemmatization were needed, for instance "ed" → "e": *health-based → health + base*. For Russian we defined a set of 15 rules to transform the left component and 14 rules to transform the right component. In the example above, the rule *"o" → ""* can be applied to the 3rd segmentation candidate: *vetro → vetr*.

If the rules are not available or not sufficient to cover all modifications, the potential lemmas are proposed using a similarity measure. We use normalized Levenshtein distance (Frunza and Inkpen, 2009) as similarity measure. Thus, *vetr* is not an independent word, and some candidate lemmas were found: *veter* 'wind', *veto* 'veto', and *vetka* 'branch', all with the similarity value of 0.8.

For each candidate segmentation, the lemmas for both components are matched with a lexicon and with a word list extracted from a specialized monolingual corpus. The lexicon contains a monolingual dictionary filtered by POS and combined with a list of neoclassical roots and prefixes to process neoclassical compounds. In this work, we kept only nouns, adjectives, verbs and adverbs in the lexicon to reduce prospective errors, even if we are aware that compound components can belong to other POS (pronouns, numerals), but in the languages that we investigated such formations are minor. Then, the segmentation score is calculated (see below).

After that we try to split the right side component further in a recursive manner, and so on up to a certain level. This level is a parameter corresponding to the maximum expected number of components, for instance:

EN kiloelectronvolt
kiloelectronvolt $\rightarrow$ kilo + electronvolt
electronvolt $\rightarrow$ electron + volt

Finally, the algorithm returns a top 5 of the best segmentations ordered by their score. For RU ветротурбина the output is:

veter turbina 0.81
veto turbina 0.8
vetka turbina 0.8

The correct split is *veter* 'wind' + *turbina* 'turbine', and indeed it has the best score given by the program.

3.2 Score Calculation

At each level of segmentation recurrence (at the first level the word is divided into 2 components, at the second level into 3 components and so on), the segmentation score is calculated as follows:

$$Score(segm) = \begin{cases} \frac{Score(compA)+Score(compB)}{2} & \text{if exact match} \\ \frac{Score(compA)+Score(compB)}{nbComp} & \text{otherwise} \end{cases}$$

where *nbComp* is the number of components in the word at this level of recurrence. "Exact match" means that all components are found "as is" in the dictionary or corpus. We consider that two-part segmentations are more frequent and more plausible than those containing three and more parts, that is why we favor the splits into two components. For example for the RU ветроколеса vetrokolesa (plural form of 'windwheel'):

Correct split is vetro.kolesa = veter 'wind' + koleso 'wheel'

$$Score(vetro + kolesa) = \frac{Score(veter) + Score(koleso)}{2}$$

Incorrect split is vetro.ko.lesa = veter 'wind' + ko 'co-, prefix' + les 'wood'

$$Score(vetro + ko + lesa) = \frac{Score(veter) + \frac{Score(ko)+Score(les)}{2}}{3}$$

An exception occurs for the splits in which the components exactly match the dictionary or corpus (e.g. EN *kiloelectronvolt*). These splits are realistic and we do not penalize them dividing by *nbComp*.

$$Score(kilo + electron + volt) = \frac{Score(kilo) + \frac{Score(electron)+Score(volt)}{2}}{2}$$

This way of calculating the segmentation score at each splitting level corresponds also to the theoretical principle defended by Benveniste (1974) and that we share: a compound word is always formed by two components. Among these two components, one can be a compound itself, but even in this case only two components take part in a compound formation. However, we have noticed in a separate experiment that the score obtained in such a way is rather close to the arithmetic mean of the component scores.

The score of a component is calculated by a linear interpolation:

$$Score(comp) = \alpha\ sim(comp, lemma) + \beta\ inDico + \gamma\ inCorpus + \delta\ DSpec \quad (1)$$

where *sim(comp,lemma)* means similarity between the component and a candidate lemma (from 0 to 1), *inDico* and *inCorpus* indicate the existence of the lemma in the lexicon and in the corpus (0 or 1), *DSpec* means domain specificity value for this lemma (see below). The sum of coefficients α, β, γ and δ is 1.

If a lemma in the lexicon is neoclassical, which means it does not occur individually in the corpus, we assign it the value *inCorpus* = 1, otherwise the score would be penalizing for all neoclassical compounds. The coefficients α, β, γ and δ are parameters and should be learned for each language using a small amount of training data (about a hundred of compounds per language).

3.3 Domain specificity

Since we are dealing with specialized vocabularies, we exploit the notion of domain specificity of a lexical unit, or in other terms, the relevance of the lexical unit for a given domain. Our domain specificity is based on Ahmad's "weirdness ratio" (Ahmad et al., 1992) which is calculated as the ratio between the term frequency in a specialized corpus and the term frequency in a general corpus. As we use a linear interpolation formula, each component of the sum should be between 0 and 1. So we normalize a weirdness ratio of a lemma dividing it by the maximum weirdness ratio found for this specialized corpus.

Domain specificity helps to disambiguate splitting variants. So, for our Russian example ветротурбина *vetroturbina*, we would like to rank the analysis *veter turbina* better than *veto turbina* or *vetka turbina*, and we rely on the fact that the word *veter* 'wind' is more specific for the given wind energy domain than the words *veto* 'veto' and *vetka* 'branch'.

Our method can also be used to process general language compounds. In this case, one should exploit a list of the words extracted from a general language corpus, with their relative frequency in this corpus instead of the domain specificity list extracted from a specialized corpus.

3.4 Training phase

The training phase consists of two steps: optimizing the coefficients used for component scoring, and defining a score threshold to recognize whether an out-of-dictionary word is a compound.

Firstly, for a given language we train our algorithm on a certain number of words annotated with their segmentations (training dataset) in order to find the best coefficients α, β, γ and δ (see equation (1)). We try all the possible coefficients from 0 to 1 with a step of 0.1 (the sum of all coefficients equals one) and we retain the combination that results in the highest recall and precision. In this step, the parameters giving the highest recall are generally the same as the ones giving the best precision.

Recall for Top N is calculated as the ratio between the number of words that have a correct split among N segmentations ranked as the best ones by the algorithm and the total number of analysed compounds:

$$Recall = \frac{nbSegmentedCorrectly}{nbCompounds} \quad (2)$$

Precision for Top N is calculated as the ratio between the number of words having a correct split among N segmentations ranked as the best ones by the algorithm and the number of words split by the algorithm:

$$Precision = \frac{nbSegmentedCorrectly}{nbSegmented} \quad (3)$$

Note that the denominator here is the number of words which were split, and not the number of all candidates produced.

Secondly, we apply again the same algorithm with the selected coefficients to a training dataset. The current objective is to determine an optimal score threshold over which the given word is probably a compound. To do that, we try all the thresholds from 0 to 1 with a step of 0.05 and calculate recall and

Language	Specialized Corpus	General Corpus	Dictionary	NCP-list
EN	314,549	5,001,609	145,542	437
RU	323,929	109,115,810	526,876	132

Table 1: Resources Statistics

precision for Top 1 and Top 5 of segmentations ranked as the best ones by the algorithm and with a score higher than this threshold.

The user can therefore choose the threshold that he considers as optimal depending on the target application. For instance, for lexicon acquisition task splitting precision will be more important than recall, whereas for the supervised translation task splitting recall may turn out more important. In this work, we optimize the threshold for a better precision. This allows us to compare the results to those of a state-of-the-art method (Koehn and Knight, 2003) which privileges precision rather than recall.

4 Experiments and Results

We use a unified strategy for the two major types of compounds, native and neoclassical. We also consider in our experiments some prefixed words. Standard prefixation is, of course, a subtype of derivation, and not of compounding. However, in some boundary cases it is difficult to catch the difference between prefixed formations and neoclassical or native compounds: compare prefix *bi-* to neoclassical root *uni-* according to Béchade (1992). Moreover, from the operational point of view, some prefixed words can be split in the same manner as compounds.

4.1 Data

Table 1 summarizes the size of the resources used in this work. Wind Energy corpora[3] were crawled from Web pages by means of Babouk (Groc, 2011), a tool dedicated to automatic compilation of domain-specific corpora, with the use of a key-term list. To compute the domain specificity of a term, we needed its frequency in the general language corpus. For the English language, we used a subpart of the *New York Times* corpus [4]. For Russian, we used a frequency list computed from The Russian National Corpus[5].

Concerning the dictionaries, we exploited the monolingual parts of the following bilingual general language dictionaries: FR-EN from the ELRA catalogue[6] for the English part, RU-EN from *English-Russian full dictionary*[7] for the Russian part.

To obtain the lists of neoclassical roots and prefixes, we firstly took the English and Russian equivalents of neoclassical elements enumerated in (Béchade, 1992). Secondly, we completed these lists with some prefixes of Latin, Greek or another origin that have equivalent in numerous languages (co-, pre-, post-, trans-, etc.). For English we consulted publicly available morpheme translation tables[8]. We will refer to this source as *NCP-list*.

We extracted from the specialized corpus a lexicon which contains only the words that (1) are either nouns or adjectives, because most compounds belong to these two categories (about 80% according to cross-language study reported in (Scalise and Fabregas, 2010)); (2) have frequencies greater than 2; (3) are 6 characters and more long; and (4) do not appear in the general language dictionary used. We applied these criteria to eliminate the words that are not compounds in order not to split them. For POS filtering, TreeTagger [9] was used.

The lexicons were randomly sorted and manually annotated until we obtained between 200 and 300 compounds. Each compound word was annotated with the correct segmentation(s), other words were marked as non-compounds. The annotated lexicons were then divided into two parts: a training dataset

[3]http://www.lina.univ-nantes.fr/?Ressources-linguistiques-du-projet.html
[4]http://catalog.ldc.upenn.edu/LDC2008T19.
[5]http://corpus.leeds.ac.uk/serge/frqlist/rnc-modern-lpos.num.html
[6]http://catalog.elra.info/product_info.php?products_id=667
[7]http://dicto.org.ru/xdxf.html
[8]http://www.lina.univ-nantes.fr/?Linguistic-resources-from-the,1676.html
[9]http://www.cis.uni-muenchen.de/~schmid/tools/TreeTagger/

Language	No. of lemmas	No. of compounds	Compound rate
		Training dataset	
EN	404	106	27%
RU	485	116	24%
		Test dataset	
EN	401	100	25%
RU	700	170	24%

Table 2: Extracted Lexicon Size and Compound Rate

used to train our system and a test dataset used to evaluate the splitting quality. Table 2 shows the lexicon sizes for each language, as well as the number of compounds found.

4.2 Experiments

The application of our method to the training data allowed us to obtain the parameters required for splitting algorithm (see Table 3). The selected coefficients were then used to analyse a test dataset for each language. The evaluation in terms of recall, precision, and F-measure is presented in Table 4.

The results vary according to the language. For Russian the precision turns out to be higher than for English: 81% for Top 1 and 82% for Top 5 for Russian against 74% for Top 1 and 78% for Top 5 for English. However, the recall is much higher for English than for Russian: 87% for Top 1 and 91% for Top 5 against 52% for Russian. It can be explained by the abundance of component modifications in the latter and by the lack of correct lemmatization for many terms. We can also notice that for Russian the gain obtained in the Top 5 of segmentation candidates is very small compared to the Top 1, which means that for this language if the correct candidate was found, it was almost always ranked as the best one.

4.3 Error Analysis

Pre-processing is very important for proper splitting and recognition of compounds and non-compounds. In our experiments lemmatization was performed by a probabilistic tool, trained on general language data, so some compound and highly specialized non-compound terms were not lemmatized correctly. The rules that we have introduced in order to deal with such cases help to properly split non-lemmatized compounds, but they do not help to recognize non-compounds. Correction of lemmatization should be done before dictionary filtering, it will enable the identification of some words as in-dictionary ones, and enable them to be kept unsplit. This will decrease the number of false segmentations and consequently improve precision.

Some false positive segmentations were due to the splitting of named entities: EN *Cambridge* split into *cam + bridge*. Named entity recognition would decrease the number of erroneous segmentations.

Among the errors intrinsic to our method, we can state those related to the use of string similarity, so certain affixes or combinations of affixes may be confused with the independent words, e.g.,

RU керосиновый 'kerosene_ADJ', non-compound word
Erroneous segmentation: kerosinovyj = kerosin 'kerosene_N' + novyj 'new'

To avoid this problem, a large set of morphemes for each morphologically rich language is needed.

4.4 Comparison to a State-of-the-art Method

We compared our method to the corpus-driven approach proposed by Koehn and Knight (2003) that became a state-of-the-art method of compound splitting. We applied it to our experimental data with the

Language	Coefficients (α β γ δ)	Score threshold
EN	0.7 0.1 0.1 0.1	0.85
RU	0.3 0.1 0.4 0.2	0.8

Table 3: Parameters Learned on the Training Dataset

Language	Top 1			Top 5		
	R	P	F	R	P	F
EN	**87**	74	**80**	**91**	78	**84**
RU	**52**	**81**	**63**	52	**82**	64

Table 4: Splitting quality evaluation in terms of R(ecall), P(precision) and F(-measure).
Highlighting corresponds to the experiments in which our method outperforms (Koehn and Knight 2003).

Language	Top 1			Top 5		
	R	P	F	R	P	F
EN	71	87	78	74	83	78
RU	48	69	57	62	68	65

Table 5: Splitting quality by (Koehn and Knight 2003) method.

usage of the same rules, stop lists and NCP-lists as we have used in our method. For the elements from the NCP-list, a corpus frequency of 1 was artificially assigned, otherwise they had no chance of being split correctly by this corpus-based method because they never independently occur in the texts. The results are presented in Table 5.

We should notice that this method can produce several segmentation candidates, including the original word kept unsplit. The unsplit word can be ranked as first, second and so on, unlike our method which first of all takes the decision whether a word is a compound or not. If for a given compound the algorithm returned the unsplit word as the first candidate, but a correct segmentation was among the first 5 candidates (e.g. *monopile* $\rightarrow$ 1) *monopile* 2) *mono pile*), we evaluated this analysis as correct for the Top 5, otherwise the evaluation would be penalizing for this method. But according to the same logic, if for a non-compound the first candidate was unsplit, and the second was split (e.g. *district* $\rightarrow$ 1) *district* 2) *di strict*), we evaluated it as correct for Top 1 and incorrect for Top 5. The consequence of such an evaluation is that the precision can be lower for the Top 5 experiments than for the Top 1 experiments, as we actually stated.

The method we proposed was more precise than Koehn and Knight's one for Russian (up to 14 points), but less precise for English (up to 13 points). Our method segmented a larger number of compounds in all experiments, except for the Top 5 for Russian. F-measure was also higher with our method (from 2 to 6 points) except for the Top 5 for Russian (1 point difference).

Koehn and Knight's method is based on corpus frequency, and it is possible to integrate linguistic rules too. Our method, besides the corpus evidence and linguistic rules, takes into account the evidence from a monolingual dictionary and the string similarity between compound elements and their lemmas.

The fact that Koehn and Knight's method does not exploit string similarity guards it against producing implausible segmentations and allows achieving, when combined with linguistic rules, a high precision, especially for the English language. However, the use of string similarity allows our method to detect some components not appearing as independent words in the texts/dictionaries even if the rules used do not cover their transformation into lemmas, cf. RU example *vetroturbina*, which was not split by Koehn and Knight's method.

Koehn and Knight's method is also known to keep some compounds unsplit if they occur more often in the corpus than their components, like the example of EN *monopile*. The neoclassical compounds also tend to remain unsplit with this method.

5 Conclusion

In this article, we have investigated the compound splitting of lexical units from specialized domains. We proposed a method for compound recognition and splitting that exploits language-independent features (corpus frequency, string similarity), lexical data (monolingual dictionary, list of neoclassical elements and prefixes) and linguistic rules. We tested this method on two languages that are not traditionally considered as highly compounding ones, but as we have seen, the specialized texts in these languages contain many compounds.

Our method turns out to be competitive with the state-of-the-art corpus-driven approach of Koehn and Knight (2003). The advantage of our method is its domain-orientation, which enables to boost correct segmentations containing specialized words into the Top 1. The use of string similarity may introduce some false positive splitting, but at the same time, it allows detection of additional components not covered by the rules. This point is particularly important to handle compounds in morphologically rich languages in which retrieval of the independent forms from compound elements is not straightforward, such as Russian. The results of both methods tested are lower for Russian than for English. This confirms that processing of Russian compounds is actually challenging for NLP systems and worth further investigating.

References

Khurshid Ahmad, Andrea Davies, Heather Fulford, and Margaret Rogers. 1992. What is a term? The semi-automatic extraction of terms from text. In *Translation Studies: An Interdiscipline*, pages 267–278, Amsterdam/Philadelphia. John Benjamins.

Hervé-D. Béchade. 1992. *Phonétique et morphologie du français moderne et contemporain*. Presses Universitaires de France.

Emile Benveniste. 1974. *Problèmes de linguistique générale*. Gallimard, Paris.

M. Braschler and B. Ripplinger. 2004. How effective is stemming and decompounding for german text retrieval. In *Information Retrieval*, pages 291–316.

A. Chen and F.C. Gey. 2001. Translation term weighting and combining translation resources in cross-language retrieval. In *Proceedings of TREC Conference*.

Chris Dyer. 2009. Using a maximum entropy model to build segmentation lattices for mt. In *Proceedings of HLT-NAACL 2009*.

0. Frunza and D. Inkpen. 2009. Identification and disambiguation of cognates, false friends, and partial cognates using machine learning techniques. In *International Journal of Linguistics*.

Clément De Groc. 2011. Babouk : Focused Web Crawling for Corpus Compilation and Automatic Terminology Extraction. In *The IEEEWICACM International Conferences on Web Intelligence*, pages 497–498, Lyon, France.

D. Hewlett and P. Cohen. 2011. Fully unsupervised word segmentation with BVE and MDL. In *Proceedings of ACL 2011*, pages 540–545, Portland, Oregon.

P. Koehn and K. Knight. 2003. Empirical methods for compound splitting. In *Proceedings of EAC 2003*, Budapest, Hungary.

K. Macherey, A.M. Dai, D. Talbot, A.C. Popat, and F. Och. 2011. Language-independent compound splitting with morphological operations. In *Proceedings of ACL 2011*, pages 1395–1404, Portland, Oregon.

Fiammetta Namer. 2009. *Morphologie, lexique et traitement automatique des langues*. Lavoisier, Paris.

N Ott. 2005. Measuring semantic relatedness of German compounds using GermaNet.

Sergio Scalise and Antonio Fabregas. 2010. Why compounding? In Sergio Scalise and Irene Vogel, editors, *Cross-disciplinary issues in compounding*, volume 311 of *Current issues in linguistic theory*, pages 1–18. John Benjamins Publishing Company, Amsterdam/Philadelphia.

Helmut Schmid, Arne Fitschen, and Ulrich Heid. 2004. SMOR: A german computational morphology covering derivation, composition, and inflection. In *Proceedings of LREC 2004*, pages 1263–1266, Lisbon, Portugal.

Sara Stymne, Nicola Cancedda, and Lars Ahrenberg. 2013. Generation of compound words in statistical machine translation into compounding languages. *Computational Linguistics*, 39(4):1067–1108.

Automatic Compound Processing: Compound Splitting and Semantic Analysis for Afrikaans and Dutch

Ben Verhoeven
CLiPS - Computational Linguistics
University of Antwerp
Antwerp, Belgium
ben.verhoeven@uantwerp.be

Menno van Zaanen
TiCC, School of Humanities
Tilburg University
Tilburg, the Netherlands
mvzaanen@uvt.nl

Walter Daelemans
CLiPS - Computational Linguistics
University of Antwerp
Antwerp, Belgium
walter.daelemans@uantwerp.be

Gerhard van Huyssteen
Centre for Text Technology (CTexT)
North-West University
Potchefstroom, South Africa
gerhard.vanhuyssteen@nwu.ac.za

Abstract

Compounding, the process of combining several simplex words into a complex whole, is a productive process in a wide range of languages. In particular, concatenative compounding, in which the components are "glued" together, leads to problems, for instance, in computational tools that rely on a predefined lexicon. Here we present the AuCoPro project, which focuses on compounding in the closely related languages Afrikaans and Dutch. The project consists of subprojects focusing on compound splitting (identifying the boundaries of the components) and compound semantics (identifying semantic relations between the components). We describe the developed datasets as well as results showing the effectiveness of the developed datasets.

1 Introduction

In many human language technology applications (e.g. machine translators and spelling checkers), many concatenatively written compounds are processed incorrectly. One of the reasons for this is that these applications rely on a predefined lexicon and the productive nature of the process of compound formation automatically results in incomplete lexicons. For example, consider the novel Afrikaans (Afr.) compound *ministerskatkis* 'treasury of a minister' that should be segmented as *minister+skatkis* **minister+treasury**. Should it be incorrectly segmented as *minister_s+kat+kis* **minister_LINK+cat+coffin**[1] (where LINK refers to a linking morpheme), one would get the (possible but improbable) interpretation 'coffin of a minister's cat'. From a technological perspective, deficiencies related to automatic compound splitting (also known as compound segmentation) are particularly problematic, since many other technologies (such as morphological analyzers, or semantic parsers) might rely on highly accurate compound splitting.

For more advanced natural language processing applications like information extraction, question answering and machine translation systems, proper semantic analysis of compounds might also be required. With semantic analysis of compounds we refer to the task of determining that the Dutch (Du.) compound *keuken+tafel* **kitchen+table** construes 'table in kitchen', while Du. *baby+tafel* **baby+table** means 'table for a baby' (and not, fatally so, *'table in a baby'). Internationally, research on automatic compound analysis has focused almost exclusively on English; very little work in this regard has been done for other languages (see section 4.1).

Concatenative compounding is a highly productive process in many languages of the world, such as West-Germanic languages (Afrikaans, Dutch, Frisian, German, and to a far lesser extent English), Nordic

[1]Note that compound boundaries are marked using a "+" sign and the start of a linking morpheme is indicated by an "_" sign.

Proceedings of the First Workshop on Computational Approaches to Compound Analysis, pages 20–30,
Dublin, Ireland, August 24 2014.

languages (Danish, Icelandic, Norwegian, and Swedish) and Modern Greek; our focus in this research is only on Afrikaans and Dutch. Next to derivation, the process of right-headed, recursive compounding is the most productive word-formation process in these two languages. While almost all parts-of-speech categories can be found as components of compounds, noun+noun compounds are by far the most frequent type, while noun+verb compounding is generally considered to be non-productive in Germanic languages (Don, 2009, p. 378). Components of a compound sometimes need to be "glued" together using linking morphemes. The occurrence of linking morphemes in Afrikaans and Dutch compounds is well-known (Neijt et al., 2010), like Afr. *besigheid_s+besluit* **business_LINK+decision** 'business decision'.

Besides regular compounding, one also finds, amongst others, phrasal compounds (e.g. Afr. *help-my-fris-lyk-hemp* **help-me-strong-look-shirt** 'gym vest'), (neo)classical compounds (e.g. Afr. *neuro+wetenskap* **neuro+science** 'neuroscience', or Du. *bio+logie* **bio+logy** 'biology'), separable verbal compounds (e.g. Du. *op+bellen* **up+call** 'to phone'), reduplicative compounds (e.g. Afr. *speel_+speel* **play_LINK+play** 'easily'), and compounding compounds (i.e. where the two left constituents are normally a phrase, but joined in a compound through the right-most constituent, e.g. Du. *onder+water+camera* **under+water+camera** 'under-water camera'). Except for the latter, none of these marginal types of compounds were considered as data for any of the systems developed in this research project.

In section 2 we provide an overview of the automatic compound processing (AuCoPro) project, which forms the background of this research. Sections 3 and 4 provide details of each of the subprojects relating to compound splitting and semantic analysis, with details about related research, the development of datasets, and our experiments. We conclude with a discussion of results and future work in section 5.

2 Overview: The AuCoPro Project

Running from 2012 to 2013, the AuCoPro project was funded by the Dutch Language Union and the Department of Arts and Culture of the South African Government in a programme to support collaborative research in human language technology between Belgium, The Netherlands and South Africa. Additional funding was provided by the South African National Research Foundation, and the European Network on Word Structure (NetWordS). The partners involved in the project were the University of Antwerp (Belgium), Tilburg University (The Netherlands), and North-West University (South Africa).

The primary aim of the project was to develop resources (including annotation protocols, and training and testing data) for the development of robust compound splitters (subproject 1), and first-generation compound analyzers (subproject 2) for Afrikaans and Dutch, through a combination of cross-language transfer (allowing technology recycling), data pooling, and various machine learning approaches. In a subpart of subproject 2 we also aimed to gain insight in compound semantics by unifying perspectives from computational semantics (Ó Séaghdha, 2008), typological studies (Scalise and Bisetto, 2009), and construction-based approaches to word-formation (specifically cognitive grammar (Langacker, 2008) and construction morphology (Booij, 2010)); the results of which can be found in Van Huyssteen (2014) and Van Huyssteen and Verhoeven (2014).

Deliverables included eight peer-reviewed publications, a technical report on annotation guidelines for compound processing, and six datasets. All deliverables are available in the open-source domain at `https://sourceforge.net/projects/aucopro`, while more information about the project is available at `http://tinyurl.com/aucopro`.

3 Compound Splitting

The aim of subproject 1 was to develop datasets that can be used to build robust compound splitters for Afrikaans and Dutch, or for a cross-lingual analysis of the use of compounds in the closely related languages Afrikaans and Dutch. Based on existing datasets containing words that are morphologically analyzed, we extracted (potential) compounds, removed unwanted morphological information, and reanalysed and corrected them.

In the AuCoPro datasets, compounds are analyzed in a shallow manner: no deep hierarchical ordering of components is performed. Compounds consisting of more than two elements are annotated by indicating the location of the boundaries, so for instance, Du. *bloem+boll_en+veld* **flower+bulb_LINK+field** 'bulb field' consists of four components, viz. *bloem*, *boll-*, *-en-*, and *veld*, without any indication of their syntagmatic relations. The parts *bloem*, *boll-* and *veld* are all simplex words, which we will call constituents. Constituents are the meaningful parts of a compound. These constituents are prototypically independent words, but in some cases affixoids (i.e. forms that are somewhere between a word and an affix in its development) can also occur in compounds (e.g. *boer* in Du. *krant_en+boer* **newspaper_LINK+farmer** 'newspaper seller' does not have the literal meaning of farmer; see Booij (2010)). In some cases a word may undergo morphophonological changes in the context of a compound. For instance, in the *bloembollenveld* example, *boll-* is an allomorph (or allograph) of *bol* 'bulb'.

As mentioned above, some compounds require linking morphemes (indicated by LINK in the examples above) to "glue" components together. Besides ordinary linking morphemes like *-e-*, *-en-*, and *-s-* (in both languages), we also defined hyphens as linking morphemes. In the orthographies of Afrikaans and Dutch in general a hyphen is used in cases of vowel collision, i.e. between compound constituents when the left-hand constituent ends on a vowel, and the right-hand constituent begins with the same vowel, for example Afr. *see_-+eend* **sea_LINK+duck** 'seaduck'.

We also mentioned above that marginal compound types such as phrasal compounds, reduplicative compounds, separable verbal compounds, etc. were not considered as part of the datasets. Similarly, we excluded synthetic compounds from the datasets when the right-hand element of a synthetic compound is a non-word (e.g. in Du. *blauw+ogig* **blue+eye-ADJR**[2] 'blue-eyed', **ogig* is not a valid independent word in Dutch). However, for this subproject we accepted and annotated compounding compounds, since they can generally be split quite easily (e.g. Afr. *drie+vlak+regering* **three+level+government** 'three-level government').

To demonstrate the effectiveness of the developed datasets, we started building and evaluating compound splitters for both Dutch and Afrikaans based on the data only. A compound splitter takes a word as input, and provides as output the input string divided into valid compound components. Note that these results are only to illustrate that these datasets can be used successfully as training data for such systems. The actual results can potentially be improved, as the systems are not optimized.

3.1 Related Research

In general, the problem of splitting compounds is found in a wide range of languages. Some of these languages show non-concatenative compound formation (i.e. compounds are written with whitespaces between constituents), such as English. Compounds in these languages fall under the umbrella term multiword expressions (MWEs), which also includes idioms and collocations. Ramisch et al. (2013) show that this is a quite active research field.

Focusing on concatenative compounding (i.e. where constituents are written conjunctively so that a compound is always written as a single string without any whitespaces), previous work on Afrikaans has been performed in the context of the development of spelling checkers (Van Zaanen and Van Huyssteen, 2002; Van Huyssteen and Van Zaanen, 2004). Van Huyssteen and Van Zaanen (2004) describe a compound splitter for Afrikaans. To our knowledge, no stand-alone compound splitter for Dutch is available. Research done in this field is over ten years old (e.g. Pohlmann and Kraaij (1996)), uses expensive resources (e.g. Ordelman et al. (2003)), does complete morphological analysis (e.g. De Pauw et al. (2004)), and/or has not been released for re-use in the open-source domain.

3.2 Dataset Development

The datasets developed during this subproject are based on compounds taken from existing (morphologically annotated) datasets. For Dutch, a few morphologically annotated datasets exist, although none focus on compounds specifically. The development of the Dutch dataset is based on the e-Lex dataset.[3]

[2] Adjectiviser.

[3] This dataset was extended with a compound dataset extracted from CELEX by Lieve Macken (LT3, UGent).

The e-Lex dataset contains words annotated with more morphological information than required for our dataset, but it also contains morphologically annotated non-compound words. After removing non-compound words (and removing duplicates), 71,274 potential Dutch compounds remained.

For Afrikaans, the situation is more difficult. No dataset containing compound boundary and linking morpheme boundary information is freely available. The Afrikaans AuCoPro dataset is based on the PUK-Protea corpus as well as the CTexT Afrikaans spelling checking lexicon (CTexT, 2005; Pilon et al., 2008). Both corpora do not describe any morphological information. To identify potential compounds, a longest string matching algorithm (Van Huyssteen and Van Zaanen, 2004) is applied. This algorithm identifies compounds by searching for known (simplex) words from the left and right ends of the potential compound, taking the possibility of the occurrence of linking morphemes into account. This algorithm seems to identify most compounds as well as some non-compounds, which resulted in a list of 77,651 potential Afrikaans compounds.

After this automatic collection and cleanup (for Dutch) and automatic identification and annotation (for Afrikaans), annotators checked each compound for correct linking morpheme and compound boundaries. For Afrikaans, seven annotators together checked 25,266 compounds. For Dutch, two annotators checked 26,000 potential compounds. In the end, this resulted in 18,497 and 21,997 true compounds for Afrikaans and Dutch respectively.

To be able to calculate inter-annotator agreement, subsets of approximately 1,000 words were annotated by pairs of annotators. For Dutch in total 6,000 words were used to calculate inter-annotator agreement and for Afrikaans 12,818 words. This leads to an average Cohen's Kappa of 98.6 and 97.6 for Afrikaans and Dutch respectively.

The annotators had access to an annotation manual (Verhoeven et al., 2014), which was developed specifically for this project. The manual is based on the annotation guidelines that were developed during the CKarma project (CTexT, 2005; Pilon et al., 2008). These initial guidelines only apply to Afrikaans, and was hence extended to handle Dutch compounds as well as more complicated cases not foreseen in the original CKarma guidelines. During the annotation process, regular discussions between the annotators took place, which resulted in changes in the data and (minor) modifications to the annotation guidelines.

3.3 Experiments

One of the reasons for creating the compound splitting datasets is to show their usefulness in the development of automatic compound splitting systems. These systems search for compound boundaries, effectively identifying the simplex words in compounds. This information is essential, for instance, when developing spelling correction systems or machine translation systems for languages that have productive compound formation processes.

As a classifier, we used the algorithm developed by Liang (1983). This system, which is used as the hyphenation method in the LaTeX typesetting system, identifies letter combinations that either allow or disallow boundary breaks. Even though the task of compound boundary detection is different from hyphenation (or syllabification), the tasks are similar enough to use the same method. Since the system is trainable, instead of hyphenation breaks, compound boundaries are provided.

Since no separate annotated gold standard test set is available, we performed leave-one-out evaluation (using all but one instance for training and the remaining instance for testing; all instances are evaluated once) using the full dataset. This approach is preferred over, for instance, 10-fold cross validation, which each time removes 10% of the training data for testing. Additionally, it does not depend on a "lucky" selection of test data from the training data, as all compounds are tested.

Evaluating the datasets using this system (which does not have any additional tuning parameters) results in classification accuracies of 88.28% and 91.48% on the word level for Afrikaans and Dutch respectively. We assume that further improvements are possible with alternative systems and parameter optimization.

4 Compound Semantics

The automatic processing of the semantics of compounds (or other complex nominals) is a topic in computational linguistics that, although it has been studied regularly in the past, cannot be considered a solved problem. Although previous research was often promising, it also had an almost exclusive focus on English noun-noun (NN) compounds. In recent years, more languages have been studied (e.g. German (Hinrichs et al., 2013) and Italian (Celli and Nissim, 2009)), and this project added Dutch and Afrikaans to the list.

It is worth noting that a number of different operationalizations of compound interpretation have been studied. The most notable are semantic classification of the constituent relation according to a limited set of semantic categories (e.g. Ó Séaghdha (2008)), and the generation of possible paraphrases for the compound that express its meaning more explicitly (Hendrickx et al., 2013). Our study adopts the classification model, in which the set of semantic relations to be predicted (the classification scheme) is crucial.

4.1 Related Research

Several attempts have been made in the past to postulate appropriate classification schemes for noun-noun compound semantics. These schemes are mainly inventory-based in that they present a limited list of predefined possible classes of semantic relations a compound can manifest.

In some cases, proposed classes are abstractly represented by a paraphrasing preposition (Lauer, 1995; Girju et al., 2005; Lapata and Keller, 2004). For example, all compounds that can be paraphrased by putting the preposition "of" between the constituents belong to the class OF, e.g. a *car door* is the 'door of a car'. Another possibility is using predicate-based classes where the relations between the constituents are not merely described by a preposition, but by definitions or paraphrasing predicates for each class. The class AGENT would contain compounds that could be paraphrased as 'X is performed by Y' (Kim and Baldwin, 2005), e.g. *enemy activity* can be paraphrased as 'activity is performed by the enemy'. Different schemes vary from 9 to 43 classes with Cohen's Kappa scores for inter-annotator agreement ranging from 52% to 62% (Barker and Szpakowicz, 1998; Girju et al., 2005; Moldovan et al., 2004; Nakov, 2008; Ó Séaghdha, 2008).

With regard to the information used by the classifier to assign the classes to the compounds (the features of a compound to be analyzed), two main approaches are available, viz. taxonomy-based methods, or corpus-based methods.

Taxonomy-based methods (also called semantic network similarity (Ó Séaghdha, 2009)) base their features on a word's location in a taxonomy or hierarchy of terms. Most of the taxonomy-based techniques use WordNet (Miller, 1995) for these purposes; especially the hyponym information in the hierarchy is used. A bag of words is created of all hyponyms and the instance vector contains binary values for each feature (the feature being whether the considered word from the bag of words is a hyponym of the constituent or not). Kim and Baldwin (2005) reached an accuracy of 53.3% using only WordNet. Other research was based on Wikipedia as a semantic network (Strube and Ponzetto, 2006).

Corpus-based methods use co-occurrence information of the constituents of the selected compounds in a corpus. The underlying idea (the distributional hypothesis) is that the set of contexts in which a word occurs, is an implicit representation of the semantics of this word (Harris, 1968). The lexical similarity measure assumes that compounds have a similar semantic interpretation when their respective constituents are semantically similar. Two compounds, for example *flour can* and *corn bag* will be considered similar if they have similar modifying constituents (*flour* and *corn*) and similar head constituents (*can* and *bag*). The co-occurrences of both constituents will be combined to calculate a measure of similarity for the entire compound. This approach implicitly uses the lexical semantic knowledge also used in taxonomy-based methods but without the need for a taxonomy. Performances of up to 64% F-score have been reached (Ó Séaghdha and Copestake, 2013).

Corpus-based and taxonomy-based methods have also been combined by several researchers. Accuracies of 58.35% (Ó Séaghdha, 2007), 73.9% (Tratz and Hovy, 2010) and even 82.47% (Nastase et al., 2006) were reported.

4.2 Dataset Development

For this project, we developed datasets of semantically annotated compounds for Afrikaans and Dutch. This section describes these new resources.

The annotation scheme and guidelines that we used as basis, were developed by Ó Séaghdha (2008) for semantic annotation of English NN compounds. For purposes of our project, some adaptations were in order, while Dutch and Afrikaans examples were added (Verhoeven et al., 2014). Ó Séaghdha (2008) describes eleven classes of compounds; six of these classes are semantically specific (see Table 1).

Class	Definition	Example
BE	The compound can be rewritten as 'N2 which is (like) (a) N1' with N1 and N2 being the two constituents nouns.	*woman doctor*
HAVE	The compound denotes some sort of possession. Part-whole compounds, typical one-to-many possession, compounds expressing conditions or properties and meronymic compounds belong here.	*car door*
IN	The compound denotes a location in time or place.	*garden party*
ACTOR	The compound denotes a characteristic event or situation and one of the constituents is a salient entity.	*enemy activity*
INST	The compound denotes a characteristic event and there is no salient entity present.	*cheese knife*
ABOUT	The compound describes a topical relation between its constituents.	*film character*

Table 1: Overview of semantically specific categories in the semantics annotation scheme.

The other five categories are less specific. The MISTAG and NONCOMPOUND categories serve to classify compounds that do not belong in the dataset. The REL class describes compounds with a clear meaning that does not belong to any of the other classes, but of which the relation between the constituents seems productive (e.g. *sodium chloride*). The LEX category is almost the same as REL, but the relation does not seem to be productive (e.g. *monkey business*). The UNKNOWN category is for correct NN compounds of which the meaning is not clear enough to annotate.

As a subpart of this subproject, we also developed an annotation protocol for nominal compounds that do not have a noun as first constituent (XN) (Verhoeven and Van Huyssteen, 2013). Such XN compounds had thus far mostly been neglected, despite the fact that they are fairly productive in some Germanic languages (although far less frequent than NN compounds). Our annotation guidelines followed the general approach of Ó Séaghdha (2008).

In the course of the project, several datasets were developed. For both Dutch and Afrikaans there were two annotation rounds for NN compounds and one smaller annotation experiment for XN compounds. An overview of the semantics data can be found in Table 2, including the average Cohen's Kappa scores.

The Dutch NN compounds were taken from the same raw compound list of 71,274 compounds described in section 3.2 above. Subsequent annotations were performed by students in linguistics at the University of Antwerp, all native speakers of Dutch. The first dataset was annotated by one student, and a subset of 500 compounds by one of the authors in order to calculate inter-annotator agreement. The second round of data was annotated by three students, with the data divided between them in such a way that we had two annotations for each compound. For the XN compound dataset, only 600 compounds were annotated.

The NN compounds for the Afrikaans dataset were taken from the CKarma list of split compounds (see section 3.2 above). The complete Afrikaans dataset was annotated by three undergraduate linguistics students, all native speakers of Afrikaans. This resulted in three annotations for each compound. With regard to the XN compound subpart, a large dataset of 4,553 compounds was annotated.

4.3 Experiments

The data from the first annotation rounds were used for semantic classification experiments that were based on those conducted by Ó Séaghdha (2008). We used the annotations made by the main annotator

language	annotation type	# items	# annotators	avg. Kappa score
Afrikaans	NN-Round1	1,449	3	53.4
Afrikaans	NN-Round2	2,328	3	37.6
Afrikaans	XN	4,553	3	33.5
Dutch	NN-Round1	1,766	2	60.0
Dutch	NN-Round2	2,000	3	51.0
Dutch	XN	600	2	48.6

Table 2: Overview of semantics data.

for each language in order to maintain his or her consistency of annotation. What follows is a description of our own experimental setup. In our classification experiment, classifiers trained by machine learning methods use feature vectors arising from a combination of the distributional hypothesis (as proposed above) with the idea of analogical reasoning. It is assumed that the semantic category of a compound can be predicted by comparing compounds with similar meanings (Ó Séaghdha, 2008).

4.3.1 Vector Creation

For every compound constituent, the co-occurrence context was calculated. For this purpose, for each instance of the constituents in the corpus, the surrounding n words (that belong to the 10,000 most frequent words of the corpus) were held in memory. The relative frequencies of these context words (the number of times the word appeared in the context of the constituent, divided by the frequency of the constituent in the corpus) for each constituent were stored.

For Dutch, the Twente News Corpus (Ordelman et al., 2007) was used. This is a 340 million word corpus of newspaper articles. For Afrikaans, we used the Taalkommissie corpus (Taalkommissie, 2011), a 60 million word corpus that consists of a variety of text genres.

A concatenation of the constituent data was used to create the instance vector. This is a new but very simple technique of composition whereby each instance vector thus contains the relative frequencies for the 1,000 most frequent words for each constituent (hence 2,000 per compound). Compounds of which one or both of the constituents did not appear in the corpus were excluded from the data.

The classification experiment dealt with those compounds that were annotated with a semantically specific category. This means that only compounds with the category tags BE, HAVE, IN, INST, ACTOR and ABOUT were used for the experiments. The final vector set for Afrikaans contained 1,439 compounds, while the final vector set for Dutch had 1,447 compounds.

4.3.2 Results

As machine learning method, we used the SMO algorithm, which is WEKA's (Witten et al., 2011) support vector machines (SVM) implementation, in a 10-fold cross-validation setup.

Since this was the first research on both Dutch and Afrikaans (Verhoeven et al., 2012), we assumed a majority baseline which represents the accuracy that can be obtained by always guessing the most frequent class as the output class. For Dutch, this baseline is 29.5% (428 instances of class IN on a total of 1,447 compounds) (Verhoeven, 2012). For Afrikaans, this baseline is 28.2% (407 instances of class ABOUT on a total of 1,439 instances).

The outcome of these experiments showed that the semantic relation between compound constituents in Dutch and Afrikaans can be learned using our simple new composition method of concatenating the constituent vectors into a compound vector. F-scores of 47.8 (Dutch) and 51.1 (Afrikaans) were achieved using the counts of three context words left and right of the constituent for computing their semantic representation. The approach turned out to be robust for varying sizes of context (different numbers of context words), as well as for the way corpus counts were done: on either lemmas or word forms (Verhoeven, 2012; Verhoeven and Daelemans, 2013). Our results are a good improvement of our baselines, and provide a baseline for future research.

4.3.3 WordNet-based method for Afrikaans

In another subpart of this subproject, we experimented with an alternative approach, namely to use the Afrikaans WordNet (CTexT, 2011) to infer compound semantics of Afrikaans compounds (Botha et al., 2013). We followed the same approach as Kim and Baldwin (2005), and achieved precision results similar to the general approach described above. i.e. 50.49% using the Afrikaans WordNet, vs. 50.80% reported by Verhoeven et al. (2012). However, recall was much worse: 29.27% in this approach, vs. 51.60% using the other approach. This poor recall can be attributed to the small size of the Afrikaans WordNet, which only contains 10,045 synsets, compared to 115,424 synsets in the Princeton WordNet (Miller, 1995). We therefore conclude that a WordNet-approach holds much promise, on the premise that the WordNet is large enough to ensure good coverage.

5 Discussion

We described machine learning approaches to the segmentation and semantic interpretation of compounds in Dutch and Afrikaans, two related languages where concatenative compounding is a highly productive morphological process. Success of machine learning approaches to any natural language processing task is based on the presence of sufficient high quality training data and relevant information sources allowing the classification problem to be solved.

For compound splitting, high annotator agreement in the annotation of the training data and high generalization accuracy could be obtained for both languages using a statistical pattern induction method working on the orthography of the input compounds, without need for other information sources. Further improvement can be achieved here with more and richer training data. Other methods for sequence learning could lead to further improvements as well, although Liang's method (1983) turns out to be a strong algorithm for this task.

The task of compound interpretation is much more difficult, both for people (who reached relatively low annotation agreement for both languages) and for machine learners, suggesting that crucial information is missing in the semantic representations we used for our compound constituents. Nevertheless, also for this task, we were able to set a standard, well above baseline, for future work in compound interpretation for Dutch and Afrikaans. Further improvement can potentially be found in many directions: more fine-grained and more learnable semantic relation types, more consistently annotated training data (and much more of it from different domains), and better semantic representations for the constituents, for example using deep learning (Mikolov et al., 2013).

Acknowledgments

The AuCoPro project was funded through a research grant from the Nederlandse Taalunie (Dutch Language Union) and the South African Department of Arts and Culture (DAC), as well as grants from the South African National Research Foundation (NRF) (grant number 81794), and the European Network on Word Structure (NetWordS) (European Science Foundation) (Grant number: 5570). Views expressed in this publication cannot be ascribed to any of these funding organizations.

We would also like to acknowledge the contributions of numerous students and colleagues, including Zandré Botha, Roald Eiselen, Joanie Liversage, Benito Trollip, Nanette van den Bergh (North-West University); Natasja Loyens, Maxim Baetens, Frederik Vaassen (University of Antwerp); Chris Emmery, Suzanne Aussems (Tilburg University).

References

Ken Barker and Stan Szpakowicz. 1998. Semi-Automatic Recognition of Non- Modifier Relationships . *Proceedings of the 17th International Conference on Computational Linguistics*, pages 96–102.

Geert Booij. 2010. *Construction Morphology*. Oxford University Press, Oxford.

Zandré Botha, Roald Eiselen, and Gerhard van Huyssteen. 2013. Automatic compound semantic analysis using wordnets. In *Proceedings of the Twenty-Fourth Annual Symposium of the Pattern Recognition Association of South Africa*, Johannesburg, South Africa.

Fabio Celli and Malvina Nissim. 2009. Automatic Identification of Semantic Relation in Italian complex nominals. In *Proceedings of the Eighth International Conference on Computational Semantics (IWCS-8)*, Tilburg, The Netherlands.

CTexT. 2005. CKarma (C5 KompositumAnaliseerder vir Robuuste Morfologiese Analise). [C5 Compound Analyser for Robust Morphological Analysis]. Centre for Text Technology (CTexT), North-West University, Potchefstroom, South Africa.

CTexT. 2011. Afrikaans WordNet. Centre for Text Technology (CTexT), North-West University, Potchefstroom, South Africa.

Guy De Pauw, Tom Laureys, Walter Daelemans, and Hugo Van Hamme. 2004. A Comparison of Two Different Approaches to Morphological Analysis of Dutch. In *Proceedings of the Workshop of the ACL Special Interest Group on Computational Phonology (SIGPHON)*, Barcelona, Spain.

Jan Don. 2009. IE, Germanic: Dutch. In Rochelle Lieber and Pavol Štekauer, editors, *The Oxford Handbook of Compounding*, pages 370–385. Oxford University Press, Oxford, UK.

Roxana Girju, Dan Moldovan, Marta Tatu, and Daniel Antohe. 2005. On the semantics of noun compounds. *Computer Speech and Language*, 19:479–496.

Zellig Harris. 1968. *Mathematical structures of language*. Interscience, New York.

Iris Hendrickx, Zornitsa Kozareva, Preslav Nakov, Diarmuid Ó Séaghdha, Stan Szpakowicz, and Tony Veale. 2013. SemEval-2013 Task 4: Free Paraphrases of Noun Compounds. In *Proceedings of the Seventh International Workshop on Semantic Evaluation (SemEval 2013)*, pages 138–143, Atlanta, Georgia, USA. Association for Computational Linguistics.

Erhard Hinrichs, Verena Henrich, and Reinhild Barkey. 2013. Using Part-Whole Relations for Automatic Deduction of Compound-internal Relations in GermaNet. *Language Resources and Evaluation*, 24(3):363–372.

Su Nam Kim and Timothy Baldwin. 2005. Automatic Interpretation of Noun Compounds Using WordNet Similarity. *Wall Street Journal*, pages 945–956.

Ronald Langacker. 2008. *Cognitive Grammar: A Basic Introduction*. Oxford University Press, New York.

Mirella Lapata and Frank Keller. 2004. The Web as a Baseline: Evaluating the Performance of Unsupervised Web-based Models for a Range of NLP Tasks. In *Proceedings of the Human Language Technology Conference of the North American Chapter of the Association for Computational Linguistics*, pages 121–128. Association for Computational Linguistics, Boston.

Mark Lauer. 1995. *Designing Statistical Language Learners: Experiments on Noun Compounds*. Ph.D. thesis, Macquarie University.

Franklin Mark Liang. 1983. *Word Hy-phen-a-tion by Com-put-er*. Ph.D. thesis, Stanford University, Stanford, USA.

Tomas Mikolov, Wen-tau Yih, and Geoffrey Zweig. 2013. Linguistic regularities in continuous space word representations. In *Proceedings of NAACL-HLT*, pages 746–751.

George Miller. 1995. WordNet: a lexical database for English. *Communications of the ACM*, 38(11):39–41.

Dan Moldovan, A Badulescu, Marta Tatu, Daniel Antohe, and Roxana Girju. 2004. Models for the Semantic Classification of Noun Compounds. In *Proceedings of the HLT-NAACL Workshop on Computational Lexical Semantics*, pages 60–67. MA: Association for Computational Linguistics, Boston.

Preslav Nakov. 2008. Noun Compound Interpretation Using Paraphrasing Verbs: Feasibility Study. In *Proceedings of the 13th International Conference on Artificial Intelligence: Methodology, Systems, Applications (AIMSA08)*.

Vivi Nastase, Jelber Sayyad-Shirabad, Marina Sokolova, and Stan Szpakowicz. 2006. Learning Noun-Modifier Semantic Relations with Corpus-based and WordNet-based Features. In *Proceedings of the 21st National Conference on Artificial Intelligence*, pages 781–787. MA: American Association for Artificial Intelligence, Boston, aaai-06 edition.

Anneke Neijt, Robert Schreuder, and Carel Jansen. 2010. Van boekenbonnen en feëverhale: De tussenklank e(n) in Nederlands en Afrikaanse samestellingen: vorm of betekenis? [The interfix e(n) in Dutch and Afrikaans compounds: form or meaning?]. *Nederlandse Taalkunde*, 15(2):125–147.

Diarmuid Ó Séaghdha and Ann Copestake. 2013. Interpreting compound nouns with kernel methods. *Journal of Natural Language Engineering, Special Issue on the Semantics of Noun Compounds*, 19:331–356.

Diarmuid Ó Séaghdha. 2008. *Learning compound noun semantics*. Ph.D. thesis, University of Cambridge, Cambridge, UK.

Roeland Ordelman, Arjan Van Hessen, and Franciska De Jong. 2003. Compound decomposition in Dutch large vocabulary speech recognition. In *Proceedings of Eurospeech 2003*, pages 225–228, Geneva, Switzerland.

Roeland Ordelman, Franciska de Jong, Arjan van Hessen, and Hendri Hondorp. 2007. TwNC: a Multifaceted Dutch News Corpus. *ELRA Newsletter 12*, pages 3–4.

Diarmuid Ó Séaghdha. 2007. Annotating and Learning Compound Noun Semantics. In *Proceedings of the ACL 2007 Student Research Workshop*, pages 73–78. Association for Computational Linguistics, Prague.

Diarmuid Ó Séaghdha. 2009. Semantic classification with WordNet kernels. In *Computational Linguistics*, NAACL-Short '09, pages 237–240. Association for Computational Linguistics.

Sulene Pilon, Martin Puttkammer, and Gerhard Van Huyssteen. 2008. Die ontwikkeling van 'n woordafbreker en kompositumanaliseerder vir Afrikaans. *Literator*, 29(1):21–41.

Renee Pohlmann and Wesley Kraaij. 1996. Improving the precision of a text retrieval system with compound analysis. In *Proceedings of the 7th Computational Linguistics in the Netherlands (CLIN 1996)*, pages 115–129, Eindhoven, The Netherlands.

Carlos Ramisch, Aline Villavicencio, and Valia Kordoni. 2013. Introduction to the special issue on multiword expressions: From theory to practice and use. *ACM Transactions on Speech and Language Processing*, 10(2):1–10.

Sergio Scalise and Antonietta Bisetto. 2009. The classification of compounds. In Rochelle Lieber and Pavol Štekauer, editors, *The Oxford Handbook of Compounding*, pages 34–53. Oxford University Press, Oxford.

Michael Strube and Simone Paolo Ponzetto. 2006. WikiRelate! Computing semantic relatedness using Wikipedia. In *Proceedings of the 21st National Conference on Artificial Intelligence (AAAI-06)*, Boston, MA.

Taalkommissie. 2011. Taalkommissiekorpus 1.1. Taalkommissie van die Suid-Afrikaanse Akademie vir Wetenskap en Kuns. Centre for Text Technology (CTexT), North-West University, Potchefstroom, South Africa.

Stephen Tratz and Ed Hovy. 2010. A Taxonomy, Dataset, and Classifier for Automatic Noun Compound Interpretation. In *Proceedings of the 48th Annual Meeting of the Association for Computational Linguistics*, pages 678–687. Uppsala: Association for Computational Linguistics.

Gerhard Van Huyssteen and Menno Van Zaanen. 2004. Learning Compound Boundaries for Afrikaans Spelling Checking. In *Proceedings of First Workshop on International Proofing Tools and Language Technologies*, pages 101–108, Patras.

Gerhard Van Huyssteen and Ben Verhoeven. 2014. A Taxonomy for Dutch and Afrikaans Compounds. In *Proceedings of the First Workshop on Computational Approaches to Compound Analysis (ComAComA)*, Dublin, Ireland.

Gerhard Van Huyssteen. 2014. Morfologie. In Wannie Carstens and Nerina Bosman, editors, *Kontemporêre Afrikaanse Taalkunde*, pages 171–208. Van Schaik Uitgewers, Pretoria, South Africa.

Menno Van Zaanen and Gerhard Van Huyssteen. 2002. Improving a Spelling Checker for Afrikaans. In *Computational Linguistics in the Netherlands 2002-Selected Papers from the Thirteenth CLIN Meeting*, page 143156, Groningen, the Netherlands.

Ben Verhoeven and Walter Daelemans. 2013. Semantic Classification of Dutch Noun-Noun Compounds: A Distributional Semantics Approach. *CLIN Journal*, 3:2–18.

Ben Verhoeven and Gerhard Van Huyssteen. 2013. More Than Only Noun-Noun Compounds: Towards an Annotation Scheme for the Semantic Modelling of Other Noun Compound Types. In *Proceedings of the 9th Joint ISO - ACL SIGSEM Workshop on Interoperable Semantic Annotation*, Potsdam, Germany.

Ben Verhoeven, Walter Daelemans, and Gerhard B. Van Huyssteen. 2012. Classification of noun-noun compound semantics in Dutch and Afrikaans. In *Proceedings of the Twenty-Third Annual Symposium of the Pattern Recognition Association of South Africa (PRASA 2012)*, pages 121–125, Pretoria, South Africa.

Ben Verhoeven, Gerhard Van Huyssteen, Menno Van Zaanen, and Walter Daelemans. 2014. Annotation guidelines for compound analysis. *CLiPS Technical Report Series (CTRS)*, 5.

Ben Verhoeven. 2012. A computational semantic analysis of noun compounds in Dutch. Master's thesis, University of Antwerp, Antwerp, Belgium.

Ian Witten, Eibe Frank, and Mark Hall. 2011. *Data Mining: Practical Machine Learning Tools and Techniques (Google eBook)*. Elsevier.

A Taxonomy for Afrikaans and Dutch Compounds

Gerhard B van Huyssteen
Centre for Text Technology
North-West University
Potchefstroom, South Africa
gerhard.vanhuyssteen@nwu.ac.za

Ben Verhoeven
CLiPS - Computational Linguistics
University of Antwerp
Antwerp, Belgium
ben.verhoeven@uantwerpen.be

Abstract

The linguistic categorisation of compounds dates back to some of the earliest work in linguistics. The cross-linguistic compound taxonomy of Bisetto and Scalise (2005), later refined in Scalise and Bisetto (2009), is well-known in linguistics for understanding the grammatical relations in compounds. Although this taxonomy has not been used extensively in the field of computational linguistics, it has the potential to influence choices with regard to compound annotation and understanding in natural language processing. For example, their 2005 taxonomy formed the basis for the large-scale, multilingual database of compounds, called CompoNet. The aim of this paper is to examine their latest taxonomy critically, especially with a view on rigorous implementation in computational environments (e.g. for the morphological annotation of compounds). We propose a number of general improvements of their taxonomy, as well as some language-specific refinements.

1 Introduction

The CompoNet database[1] is a large database of compounds from 27 different languages, which was developed at the Department of Foreign Languages of the University of Bologna, in collaboration with native speaker linguists. The database can be used to study compounding of a given language, of a given family (e.g. Germanic, Slavic, etc.), and compounding in general from a typological perspective. Fields in the database include, inter alia, the compound and its part-of-speech (POS) category; the components in the compound and their respective POS categories; the structure of the compound (e.g. [N+N]); whether it is endocentric or exocentric, and an indication of the position of the categorial and semantic head; some inflectional information (plural and gender); glosses; and the classification category of the compound.

With regard to the latter, the well-known classification taxonomy of Bisetto and Scalise (2005) is used (see Figure 1). This classification scheme is based on the view that the grammatical relations between the components of a compound are similar to those in syntactic constructions, *viz.* subordinate, attributive, and coordinate relations. In addition, each of these types can be endocentric or exocentric, depending of the presence (endocentric) or absence (exocentric) of a head constituent.

In a project on automatic compound processing (the AuCoPro project; see http://tinyurl.com/aucopro), we investigated various aspects related to the computational processing of compounds (Verhoeven et al., 2014). In a specific subpart of this project, we aimed to gain more insight in compound semantics in general by drawing from perspectives from computational semantics (i.e. Ó Séaghdha, 2008), typological studies (e.g. Lieber, 2009a; Scalise & Bisetto, 2009), and

[1] http://componet.sslmit.unibo.it/

Proceedings of the First Workshop on Computational Approaches to Compound Analysis, pages 31–40,
Dublin, Ireland, August 24 2014.

construction-based approaches to word-formation (i.e. cognitive grammar (Langacker, 2008) and construction morphology (Booij, 2010)). In addition, we specifically wanted to add Afrikaans compounds to the CompoNet database (as Afrikaans was not included in the original CompoNet project), as well as revise the existing Dutch compounds in CompoNet (based on the insights of the AuCoPro project). As a first phase, we made 56 changes to the Dutch database (mostly correcting minor spelling and classification errors, as well as adding a few additional, prototypical examples), and added 144 Afrikaans compounds to the database (compared to a total of 188 Dutch compounds; the 144 Afrikaans compounds were representative of all part-of-speech categories that can be found in Afrikaans compounds).

However, soon after the project commenced, we encountered some limitations with the original CompoNet annotation guidelines, specifically with regard to the classification of compounds. In Section 2 we give an overview of these problems, and discuss some recent literature on the classification of compounds. In Section 3 we describe our solution to these limitations by postulating a classification scheme that would be suitable for rigorous implementation in computational environments (e.g. for the morphological annotation of compounds). We conclude this paper with a discussion of future research.

2 Previous work

In a publication of this nature, it is impossible to discuss all previous research, or even the details of some of the literature influencing our own taxonomy for Afrikaans and Dutch (see Section 3); suffice to point to the overview and summary provided by Scalise and Bisetto (2009), as well as applications of their framework by Lieber (2009a, 2009b). In the remainder of this section we therefore only focus on those aspects that influenced our own taxonomy.

During the initial phase of the project, we encountered a number of stumbling-blocks with regard to the annotation guidelines. As indicated above, compound classification in the CompoNet database is based on Bisetto and Scalise (2005) (see Figure 1). However, since then, Scalise and Bisetto (2009) have revised their original taxonomy (see Figure 2), and the dilemma was therefore that we could not take cognisance of these new insights (e.g. the distinction between root and verbal-nexus compounds, or between attributives and appositives), since we had to stay as close as possible to the original annotation guidelines for purposes of cross-lingual compatibility. Table 1 provides a summary of some of the most important notions in Scalise and Bisetto's (2009) taxonomy, some additional remarks by Lieber (2009a, 2009b), and examples provided by them. Other summaries of their framework include Arcodia et al. (2009); Arnaud and Renner (2014); Vercellotti and Mortensen (2012).

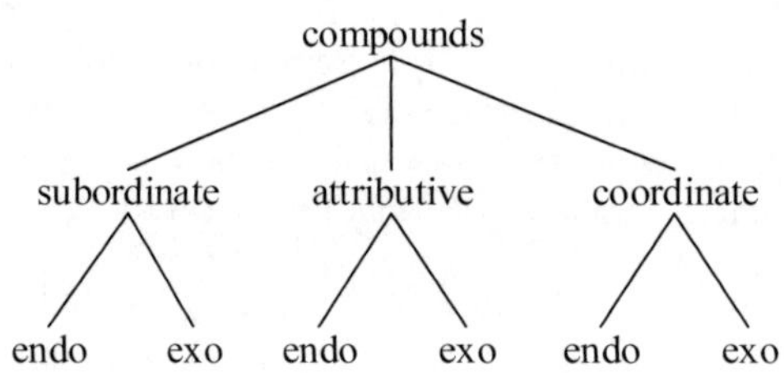

Figure 1. Compound taxonomy of Bisetto and Scalise (2005)

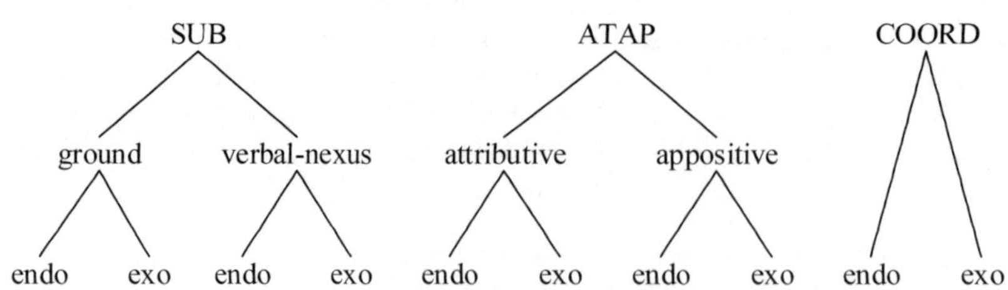

Figure 2. Compound taxonomy of Scalise and Bisetto (2009)

Concept	Key definitional aspects	Examples
Subordinate	• Components share a head-complement relation (subordination) • Argumental relation between components (Lieber, 2009a: 93) • At least one of the features of the head constituent is to match the encyclopaedic features that characterise the non-head • Includes synthetic compounds (Lieber, 2009b: 359), and neoclassical compounds • Among the most widely attested of compound types (specifically endocentric; Lieber, 2009a: 93)	See below under "Ground subordinate" and "Verbal-nexus subordinate"
Ground subordinate	• Corresponds to root/primary compounds • Lexemes can be both simple and complex • When complex and includes a verb, it is incapable of influencing the interpretation of the compound [no examples provided] • Semantic relation between constituents is influenced by semantico-encyclopaedic information • NN compounds with an 'of' relation (Lieber, 2009a: 88), but also if they have a (quasi-)argumental relation (e.g. *cookbook author*) (Lieber, 2009b: 359)	*windmill* (endocentric) *mushroom soup* (endocentric) *love story* (endocentric) *steam boat* (endocentric) *coffee cup* (endocentric)
Verbal-nexus subordinate	• Corresponds to secondary/syntactic compounds • Presence of verb (or any other deverbal constituent) as head • Verbs select the non-head semantically, be it an argument (*bookseller*) or a complement/adjunct (*street seller*) • Quintessential example is synthetic compound (Lieber, 2009a: 88)	*truck driver* (endocentric) *cost containment* (endocentric) *city employee* (endocentric) *pickpocket* (exocentric) *killjoy* (exocentric) *cut-throat* (exocentric)
Attributive	• Non-head (often an adjective) expresses a quality of the head [often a noun] (i.e. head is modified by a non-head expressing a 'property' of the head) • The non-head fulfils at least one of the encyclopaedic features of the head; it has an 'adjectival' function • Clear argumental relationship between constituents lacks (Lieber, 2009b: 359) • Default semantic type (Lieber, 2009a: 97) • Most frequently attested in the languages of the world (Lieber, 2009a: 97)	*high-school* (endocentric) *blue-eyed* (endocentric) *blue cheese* (endocentric) *atomic bomb* (endocentric) *redskin* (exocentric) *greenhouse* (exocentric) *freelance* (exocentric)
Appositive	• Non-head expresses a property of the head by means of a noun acting as an attribute • Noun plays an attributive role and is often interpreted metaphorically • Non-head can also be a verb [when the head is an adjective] • NN compounds cannot be paraphrased with 'of' (Lieber, 2009a: 88)	*snail mail* (endocentric) *swordfish* (endocentric) *mushroom cloud* (endocentric) Du. *druipnat* (endocentric)
Coordinate	• Constituents with an 'and' relation • Two semantic heads, but only one act as categorial head • Could be additive (*Baden-Württemberg*), or redundant (*palm tree*) • Coordinates could be, *inter alia*, reduplicates (It. *lecca-lecca* 'lolly-pop')	*bittersweet* (endocentric) *poet-doctor* (endocentric) *woman doctor* (endocentric) *Austria-Hungary* (exocentric) *mother-child* (exocentric) *north-east* (exocentric)

Table 1. Verbatim summary of Scalise and Bisetto (2009) with additional remarks by Lieber (2009a, 2009b), and our remarks in square brackets

There are two significant differences between these two taxonomies: the label ATAP (ATtributive-APpositive) is introduced in the 2009 version; and a new categorisation level is introduced in the 2009 version to make a distinction between root and verbal-nexus compounds. With the introduction of the "artificial" ATAP label (placed on the same hierarchical level as subordinate and coordinate compounds) as a superordinate category for attributive and appositive compounds, Scalise and Bisetto (2009) lost some "correctness". In the new taxonomy attributives and appositives are therefore on the same categorisation level as verbal-nexus and ground compounds, which, in our opinion, is incorrect. (Fábregas and Scalise (2012) later replace attributive compounds to its original hierarchical level, and then distinguish between two types of attributive compounds, *viz.* true attributives, and appositives. Also see Arnaud and Renner (2014), and Vercellotti and Mortensen (2012: 572) for a critique of the categorisation levels used by Scalise and Bisetto (2009).)

The only annotation protocol available for CompoNet is the article by Bisetto and Scalise (2005), as well as some notes for some of the languages on the CompoNet website (only available to registered users). In our experience, these guidelines were not always explicit or elaborate enough (see also Vercellotti and Mortensen, 2012: 547), and in addition, were sometimes difficult to interpret given other discussions in the literature (notably Fábregas and Scalise, 2012; Lieber, 2009a, 2009b; Scalise and Bisetto, 2009). Two examples suffice. Firstly, in Table 1 we indicated that Scalise and Bisetto (2009: 48-49) distinguish between subordinate and attributive compounds by the manner in which the head selects the non-head: in subordinate compounds "at least one of the features of the head constituent is **to match** the encyclopaedic features that characterise the non-head" (with *apple cake* as an example), while in attributive compounds "the non-head **fulfils** at least one of the encyclopaedic features of the head" (with *snail mail* as an example). In our opinion, this should be the other way round: in SNAIL and MAIL the property SLOW provides the **match** between the two constituents, whereas APPLE **fulfils** the INGREDIENT part of the concept CAKE.

A second example that confuses, comes from Lieber (2009a): on p. 98, with regard to *dog bed* as an example of an attributive compound, she states that "there is no verbal element here, so a subordinate interpretation is ruled out". However, on p. 93 she lists *table leg* as one of the first examples of endocentric subordinate compounds, despite the fact that there is also no verbal element in *table leg*. Similarly, Vercellotti and Mortensen (2012: 549) interprets Scalise and Bisetto's (2009) differentiation between verbal-nexus and ground compounds on the basis that the former have verb-argument/adjunct relations, while the latter have *no verbs*. However, Scalise and Bisetto (2009: 51) says about ground compounds containing complex lexemes: "when they *include a verb*, this is incapable of influencing the interpretation of the compound" (our emphasis). Although examples like these might be trivial (and does not take away anything from the overall insight in the categorisation of compounds), they do cause some confusion for the annotator who is provided with these publications as annotation guidelines.

Lastly, one of the problems we had with the original taxonomy was that it was not rich enough to allow for all compound types in Afrikaans and Dutch to be categorised, or at least not powerful enough to distinguish between various kinds of compounds. For example, in the original database a separable complex verb (SCV) like the Dutch (Du.) *neer+gooien* **down+throw** 'to throw down' was categorised as an attributive compound, while it should in reality rather be categorised as "Other" (OTH), a category in CompoNet reserved for examples that do not fit any of the other categories. Other examples include the difference between synthetic compounds (like the Afrikaans (Afr.) *gras+sny-er* **grass+cut-extN** 'lawn mower'[2]) and parasynthetic compounds (Afr. *glad+maak-ing* **smooth+make-extN** 'smoothing'), compounding compounds (Du. *oude+mannen+huis* **old+men+house** 'retirement home for men'), and reduplications (Afr. *speel_-+speel* **play_LINK+play** 'easily'). This illustrates that any taxonomy should at least provide for a slot for language-specific or other marginal phenomena – an aspect we will introduce in Section 3.

3 New proposal

In motivating why they came up with a revised taxonomy, Scalise and Bisetto (2009: 49) state that, given "the evolution of science, the need has arisen to add further levels of analysis to the classification". They also invite further amendments to their newly proposed taxonomy, but warn that "anyone wanting to follow up on this issue will necessarily have to come to grips … with the diverse compound formations that populate the languages of the world" (Scalise and Bisetto, 2009: 53). In as such, our new proposal wants to suggest some refinements to the general taxonomy of Scalise and Bisetto (2009) on the one hand, and on the other hand wants to make some language-specific changes pertaining to Afrikaans and Dutch (with the possibility that it could also be applicable to other (Germanic) languages). Furthermore, it should be kept in mind that our taxonomy also has a secondary aim, namely to serve as a structure for annotation of compounds in a database like CompoNet.

Our proposed taxonomy is presented in Figure 3, while Table 2 (as an Appendix) explicates this taxonomy with construction schemas for prototypical endocentric compounds, as well as an Afrikaans example for each instance. Although only Afrikaans examples are listed, we do claim that the

---

[2] Following the conventions in CompoNet, we use the following abbreviations: extN=nominaliser; extV=verbaliser; extAdj=adjectiviser; extAdv=adverbialiser; Sw=semi-word.

taxonomy holds true for Dutch: all categorial patterns listed by De Haas & Trommelen (1993) have been accounted for in some or other way in the taxonomy. In the remainder of this section, we explain and motivate only those aspects of our taxonomy that differ from Scalise and Bisetto (2009).

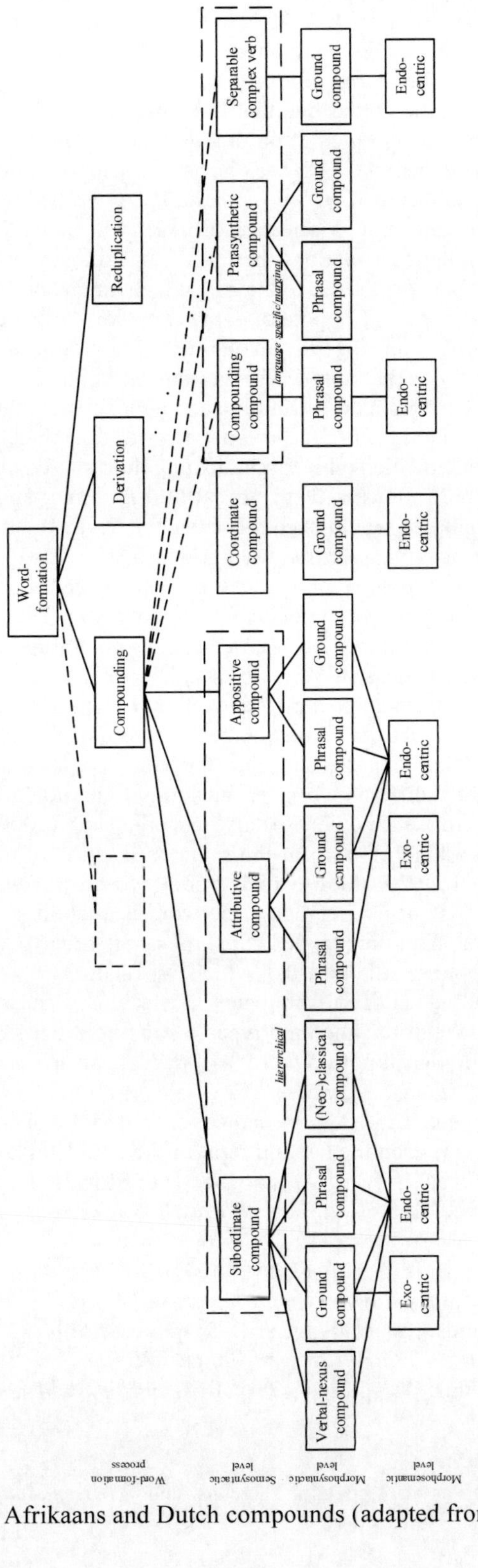

Figure 3. Taxonomy for Afrikaans and Dutch compounds (adapted from Van Huyssteen, 2014)

One of the important aspects of any taxonomy, is that taxa of the same type should be placed on the same taxonomic level/rank (e.g. *dog* and *cat* are on the same taxonomic rank), and that criteria for such ranks should be made explicit. In our taxonomy, we show that compounding, derivation, reduplication, etc., are all word-formation processes. We explicitly include reduplication here, in order to clarify that we do not consider examples like Afr. *dokter-dokter* **doctor-doctor** 'play doctor', or Du. *snel+snel* **quick+quick** 'very quick' to be compounds, as some authors like Kempen (1969) believe, but rather consider it a separate word-formation process (following Fábregas and Scalise, 2012, and Van Huyssteen, 2004). Note also the dotted line that links derivation with parasynthetic compounds, because parasynthetic compounds are formed through a derivational process: compounding by means of derivation (Booij and Van Santen, 1998: 178; see discussion below).

With regard to compounding specifically, we maintain the three taxonomic ranks of Scalise and Bisetto (2009) (unlike Vercellotti and Mortensen (2012) who added another level). On the semosyntactic level, the grammatical relations between constituents in compounds are used as classification criterion, and four types of relations are distinguished: subordinate, attributive, appositive, and coordinate. These four taxa operate on the same level of categorisation, and not like in the 2009-version of the Scalise and Bisetto taxonomy, where attributive and appositive were positioned on the same level as verbal-nexus and ground compounds. Following Vercellotti and Mortensen's (2012) insight that subordinate, attributive and appositive compounds are more similar to each other than to coordinate compounds (i.e. the latter is not hierarchical), we lump them together with a dotted line in an area marked "hierarchical" (indicating their shared characteristic).

Note also that Vercellotti and Mortensen (2012) discard the notion of appositive compounds, since: (1) it "is unclear how many languages would need this category, given the difficulty distinguishing the category"; and (2) "'appositive' is already in the literature as a type of coordinate compound" (2012: 574). We have to agree to some degree with them on both accounts, but nonetheless maintain appositive as a useful label. Compare an appositive compound like Du. *sleutel+woord* **key+word** 'keyword' with a coordinate compound like Du. *dichter-zanger* **poet-singer** 'idem'. A *sleutelwoord* is a word that is like a key, but nonetheless still a word; it is not a key that is also a word. In contrast, a *dichter-zanger* is a singer that happens to be a poet as well, but could just as well be paraphrased as a poet that happens to be a singer. Hence, we maintain that there is a difference between appositives and coordinates, with the former being right-headed, and the latter (at least semantically) dual-headed. Similarly, an appositive is subtly different from an attributive compound (and it is therefore often difficult to distinguish the two from each other; see also Arcodia et al. (2009), and Arnaud and Renner (2014)). A *sleutelwoord* is not a kind of word of the same order as a Du. *taboe+woord* **taboo+word** 'taboo word', or a Du. *mode+woord* **fashion+word** 'trendy word': a *sleutelwoord* is a word that **is like a** key, while a *taboewoord* is not like a taboo – the word **is** a taboo; a *modewoord* is not like the fashion, it **is** fashion. We maintain that appositives most often have an 'is like' metaphorical interpretation, while attributives have a literal '(that/which) is' relation.

On the semosyntactic level, we can now formulate high-level construction schemas (Booij, 2010) for each of the four major endocentric compound types, as the bold parts in (1) to (4). To illustrate, read (1) as follows: on the phonological pole, a word $[a]_{Xi}$ (*table*) can combine with another word $[b]_{Xk}$ (*leg*) to form a new word $[ab]_{Xk}$ (*table leg*), which as a whole ($_k$) should be interpreted on the semantic pole as $[\mathrm{LEG}_j \text{ of } \mathrm{TABLE}_i]_k$; note that $_i$, $_j$ and $_k$ are indices that mark the identity of constituents on the phonological and semantic poles (i.e. on the left and right of the double-arrow respectively).

(1) Subordinate compounds: $\mathbf{[[a]_{Xi}\,[b]_{Xj}]_{Xk} \leftrightarrow [SEM_j\ of\ SEM_i]_k}$
where the $_X$ of [a]=N/V/Adj/Adv/Num/P/Phrase/Sw; the $_X$ of [b]=N/Adj/V/V-extN/V-extAdj/Sw[3]

(2) Attributive compounds: $\mathbf{[[a]_{Xi}\,[b]_{Xj}]_{Xk} \leftrightarrow [SEM_j\ is\ SEM_i]_k}$
where the $_X$ of [a]=Adj/Adv/AP/Num/Phrase; the $_X$ of [b]=N/Adj

(3) Appositive compounds: $\mathbf{[[a]_{Xi}\,[b]_{Xj}]_{Xk} \leftrightarrow [SEM_j\ like\ SEM_i]_k}$
where the $_X$ of [a]=N/V/P/Phrase; the $_X$ of [b]=N/Adj

(4) Coordinate compounds: $\mathbf{[[a]_{Xi}\,[b]_{Xj}]_{Xk} \leftrightarrow [SEM_i\ and/or\ SEM_j]_k}$
where $_X$=N/V/Adj/Adv/P

---

[3] In Afrikaans, a pronoun can also act as head, as in the construction Afr. *ma-hulle* **mother-they** 'mother and them'.

On the second taxonomic rank, the morphosyntactic level, compounds are distinguished in terms of the morphosyntactic (categorial) nature of the constituents, i.e. whether it is a lexical word, a phrase, or semi-word; in (1) to (4) these constituents are indicated in italics. All four types of compounds can be formed by means of ground words (i.e. uninflected words), which could be either simplex (e.g. *gebruik* in Afr. *gebruik+sfeer* **usage+sphere** 'usage sphere'), or complex (e.g. Afr. *gebruik-er* **use-extN** 'user' in *gebruiker+vriendelik* **user+friendly** 'user friendly'). All the major word categories can function as constituents in compounds, including N, V, Adj, Adv, Num, and P.

All except coordinate compounds can take phrasal elements as non-heads; these could range from full sentences (Afr. *Sannie-gaan-weeshuis-toe-rokkie* **Sannie-goes-orphanage-to-dress** 'worn-out dress'), phrases (NP, VP, AP, PP), or phrase-like phrases (Lieber, 2009b: 363) as in some parasynthetic compounds. Only subordinate compounds can have deverbal constituents as heads where the verb selects the non-head semantically as argument or as complement/adjunct (resulting in synthetic compounds). Lastly, it seems thus far as if only subordinate compounds can have semi-words as constituents, resulting in (neo-)classical compounds.

The third taxonomic rank pertains to headedness, defined on the morphosemantic level. Without being ignorant about the ongoing debate on headedness in morphology circles, we simply maintain Scalise and Bisetto's (2009) definition and interpretation of the head as the semantic head of the compound (see also Booij, 1992). Whereas they indicate that all three major compound types can be both endocentric or exocentric (universally speaking), we claim that all compound types in Afrikaans and Dutch can be endocentric, but only the following can be exocentric:[4]

(5) Subordinate, ground: $[[a]_V\ [b]_N]_V$ (Du. *knip+oog* **snip+eye** 'to wink'), or $[[a]_V\ [b]_N]_N$ (Afr. *suip+lap* **booze+cloth** 'drunkard')

(6) Attributive, ground: $[[a]_{Adj}\ [b]_N]_N$ (Afr. *rooi+kop* **red+head** 'ginger (*derogatory*)'), or $[[a]_N\ [b]_N]_N$ (Du. *spleet+oog* **slit-eye** 'Asian person (derogatory)'[5])

Finally, another important addition to our taxonomy is the grouping of language specific/marginal cases (on the right-hand side of Figure 3). This choice should be understood in terms of the computational needs of this project, where one often needs a category for instances that do not fit the other main categories well. Such a category is currently called "Other" in CompoNet, and is used as a "dustbin" for anything that cannot be categorised as "Subordinate", "Attributive", "Appositive" or "Coordinate". However, instead of having a very vague "Other" category, we try to be precise and explicit about these language specific categories. With regard to Afrikaans and Dutch, we identify three categories, *viz.* compounding compounds (Afr. *samestellende samestellings*), parasynthetic compounds (Afr. *samestellende afleidings*), and separable complex verbs (Afr. *samekoppelings*).

Compounding compounds are compounds that are formed with a noun as head, and either a NP (Adj+N, or Num+N) or PP (P+N) as non-head. Note that this is a specific kind of construction, and should as such not be confused with recursiveness in compounding. Unlike in subordinate, attributive and appositive phrasal compounds, the NP or PP in compounding compounds can only have two constituents. Also, a binary, left-branching interpretation of the compound as a recursive compound is impossible. Compare for instance a jocular example like Du. *gescheurde+broek+hersteller* **ripped+pants+repairer** 'repairer of ripped pants'. If we would assume that *hersteller* first combined with *broek* to form *broekhersteller*, then a *gescheurde broekhersteller* would have been a 'pants repairer who was ripped'. In other words, in compounding compounds, the compound as a whole is formed by means of the usual process of compounding (Booij and Van Santen, 1998: 179). In contrast,

---

[4] Note that an example like Afr. *wag-'n-bietjie* **wait-a-bit** 'Buffalo Thorn (tree type)' should not be analysed as exocentric, since it is actually a back-formation of *wag-'n-bietjie-boom* **wait-a-bit-tree** 'Buffalo Thorn'. There is a handful of highly lexicalised phrases (written concatenatively with hyphens, indicating their word status) that are exocentric, e.g. Afr. *een-twee-drie* **one-two-three** 'quickly', or Du. *vergeet-me-niet-je* **forget-me-not-DIM** 'idem'. Most of these cases are names of plants, birds, food, etc., and in our opinion, are not productive in Afrikaans and Dutch. However, this will need to be established through future research.
Other problematic examples include highly lexicalised (metaphoric) compounds (like Du. *pad(den)+stoel* **frog+chair** 'mushroom'), or simplexes that were diachronically speaking endocentric compounds (like Afr. *hard+loop* **fast+walk** 'run', which is still today considered an endocentric attributive compound in Dutch). For our purposes we consider both these cases as simplexes, but it could also be a theme for future research.

[5] The compound *spleetoog* can also refer to a squinted eye, in which case it is endocentric.

in parasynthetic compounds, the compound is formed by means of derivation; compare for instance Du. *vijf+jaar-s* **five+year-extAdv** 'five-yearly', or Afr. *besluit+ne(e)m-ing* **decision+take-extN** 'decision making'.

Lastly, we also include separable complex verbs in our taxonomy as a language specific category, and specifically as endocentric ground compounds. There is a vast literature on whether examples like Du. *op+zoeken* **up+look** 'look up/search for', and Afr. *af+sny* **off+cut** 'cut off' should be seen as compounds or not. Suffice to point the interested reader to Booij's (2010) recent summary and discussion of the topic, and to state that we consider separable complex verbs as language specific compounds, based on the fact that they follow the same stress pattern as other compounds in Afrikaans and Dutch (i.e. main stress on the left-hand constituent).

4 Conclusion

In this paper, we have evaluated Bisetto and Scalise's (2005) and Scalise and Bisetto's (2009) compound taxonomies for purposes of revising the Dutch part of CompoNet, and to extend CompoNet by adding Afrikaans as a new language. Similar to Vercellotti and Mortensen's (2012) critique of these taxonomies, we also suggested some changes, which might actually be more of interest to linguists. However, in our case we had a very practical aim as well, namely to explicate various aspects of the framework for practical analysis and annotation of Afrikaans and Dutch data in the CompoNet database. As is illustrated by Table 2 (in the appendix), we were able to comprehensively formalise the various patterns of compounding in Afrikaans and Dutch, and in the next phase of the project we will revise the original Afrikaans and Dutch data based on our taxonomy, in order to develop two supplementary databases (not part of the official CompoNet, but still using all their fields and conventions). Such databases could in future be used for comparative research, not only between Afrikaans and Dutch, but also with other languages in the CompoNet database.

Specific topics that need to be investigated in future include phrasal compounds (e.g. if we perhaps missed some patterns, what kind of phrases occur in which kinds of compounds?), exocentric compounds (i.e. do they only occur as ground compounds, or was our data skewed?; do we really need to include exocentricity in a compounding taxonomy for Afrikaans and Dutch), and (neo-)classical compounds (i.e. are (neo-)classical compounds always subordinate compounds?). Another topic pertains to the productivity of verbal compounds. Booij (2007: 92) states that Germanic languages do not have processes of verbal compounding, but that in Frisian occasionally new NV compounds do occur; we suspect that the same might be true for Afrikaans. Other topics of comparative research on compounding in Afrikaans and Dutch include whether (and why) Afrikaans has more A+N compounds than Dutch, the controversial topic of left-headed constructions in Dutch (e.g. Du. *kabinet-Zuma* **cabinet-Zuma** vs. Afr. *Zuma-kabinet* **Zuma-cabinet** 'cabinet of (president) Zuma'), the difference of spreading of interfixes (linking morphemes), and differing stress patterns in compounding compounds in these two languages.

Acknowledgements

The Automatic Compound Processing (AuCoPro) project (http://tinyurl.com/aucopro) was funded through a research grant from the Nederlandse Taalunie (Dutch Language Union) and the South African Department of Arts and Culture (DAC), as well as grants from the South African National Research Foundation (NRF) (grant number 81794), and the European Network on Word Structure (NetWordS) (European Science Foundation) (Grant number: 5570). Views expressed in this publication cannot be ascribed to any of these funding organisations. We would also like to acknowledge the contributions of Benito Trollip, who populated the first version of the Afrikaans section in the CompoNet database. Thank you also to the anonymous reviewers for their comments and suggestions.

References

Giorgio F. Arcodia, Nicola Grandi and Fabio Montermini. 2009. Hierarchical NN compounds in a cross-linguistic perspective. *Rivista di Linguistica*, 21(1):11-33.

Pierre J.L. Arnaud and Vincent Renner. 2014. English and French $[NN]_N$ lexical units: A categorial, morphological and semantic comparison. *Word Structure*, 7(1):1-28.

Antonietta Bisetto and Sergio Scalise. 2005. The classification of compounds. *Lingue e Linguaggio,* 4(2):319-332.

Geert Booij. 1992. Compounding in Dutch. *Rivista di Linguistica,* 4:37-59.

Geert Booij. 2007. *The grammar of words*. Oxford University Press, Oxford.

Geert Booij. 2010. *Construction Morphology*. Oxford University Press, Oxford.

Geert Booij and Ariane Van Santen. 1998. *Morfologie*. Amsterdam University Press, Amsterdam.

Antonio Fábregas and Sergio Scalise. 2012. *Morphology: From Data to Theories*. Oxford University Press.

Wim De Haas and Mieke Trommelen. 1993. *Morfologisch Handboek van het Nederlands [Morphologic Handbook of Dutch]*. SDU Uitgeverij.

Walter Haeseryn, Kirsten Romijn, Guido Geerts, Jaap de Rooij & Maarten Cornelis van den Toorn. 1997. *Algemene Nederlandse Spraakkunst [ANS]*. Martinus Nijhoff, Groningen.

Willem Kempen, 1969. *Samestelling, Afleiding en Woordsoortelike Meerfunksionaliteit in Afrikaans [Compounding, Derivation and Conversion in Afrikaans]*. Nasou, Cape Town, South Africa.

Ronald Langacker. 2008. *Cognitive Grammar: A Basic Introduction*. Oxford University Press, New York.

Rochelle Lieber. 2009a. A Lexical Semantic Approach to Compounding. In Rochelle Lieber and Pavol Štekauer, editors, *The Oxford Handbook of Compounding*, pages 78-104. Oxford University Press, Oxford.

Rochelle Lieber. 2009b. IE, Germanic: English. In Rochelle Lieber and Pavol Štekauer, editors, *The Oxford Handbook of Compounding*, pages 34–53. Oxford University Press, Oxford.

Diarmuid Ó Séaghdha. 2008. *Learning compound noun semantics*. Ph.D. thesis, University of Cambridge, Cambridge, UK.

Sergio Scalise and Antonietta Bisetto. 2009. The classification of compounds. In Rochelle Lieber and Pavol Štekauer, editors, *The Oxford Handbook of Compounding*, pages 34–53. Oxford University Press, Oxford.

Gerhard Van Huyssteen. 2004. Motivating the composition of Afrikaans reduplications: a cognitive grammar analysis. In Günter Radden and Klaus-Uwe Panther, editors, *Studies in Linguistic Motivation*, pages 269-292. Mouton de Gruyter, Berlin.

Gerhard Van Huyssteen. 2014. Morfologie [Morphology]. In Wannie Carstens and Nerina Bosman, editors, *Kontemporêre Afrikaanse Taalkunde [Contemporary Afrikaans Linguistics]*, pages 171-208. Van Schaik Uitgewers, Pretoria, South Africa.

Mary Lou Vercellotti and David R. Mortensen. 2012. A classification of compounds in American Sign Language: an evaluation of the Bisetto and Scalise framework. *Morphology*, 22(4):545-579.

Ben Verhoeven, Menno van Zaanen, Walter Daelemans and Gerhard Van Huyssteen. 2014. Automatic Compound Processing: Compound Splitting and Semantic Analysis for Afrikaans and Dutch. In *Proceedings of the First Workshop on Computational Approaches to Compound Analysis (ComAComA)*, Dublin, Ireland.

Appendix

Subordinate	VerbNex	$[[a]_N [[b]_V extAdj]_{Adj}]_{Adj}$	*hand+vervaardig-de*	**hand+produce-extAdj**	hand-made
		$[[a]_N [[b]_V extN]_N]_N$	*gras+sny-er*	**grass+cut-extN**	lawn mower
		$[[a]_V [[b]_V extN]_N]_N$	*eet+sta(a)k-ing*	**eat+strike-extN**	hunger strike
		$[[a]_{Adj} [[b]_V extN]_N]_N$	*kaal+nael-er*	**naked+run-extN**	streaker
		$[[a]_{Adv} [[b]_V extAdj]_{Adj}]_{Adj}$	*dig+bebos-te*	**thick+afforest-extAdj**	thickly wooded
	G	$[[a]_N [b]_N]_N$	*tafel+poot*	**table+leg**	table leg
		$[[a]_N [b]_{Adj}]_{Adj}$	*kleur+blind*	**colour+blind**	colour blind
		$[[a]_P [b]_N]_N$	*buite+kamer*	**outside+room**	outside room
		$[[a]_{Num} [b]_N]_N$	*twee+klank*	**two+sound**	diphthong
		$[[a]_V [b]_N]_N$	*stryk+plank*	**iron+board**	ironing board
		$[[a]_N [b]_V]_V$	*raad+pleeg*	**advice+commit**	consult
	Ph	$[[a]_{VP} [b]_N]_N$	*skop-skiet-en-donder-film*	**kick-shoot-and-hit-movie**	action movie
		$[[a]_{NP} [b]_N]_N$	*kaas-en-wyn-onthaal*	**cheese-and-wine-party**	cheese and wine party
	NeoC	$[[a]_{Sw} [b]_{Sw}]_N$	*hidro+logie*	**hydro+logy**	hydrology
		$[[a]_{Sw} [b]_N]_N$	*bio+brandstof*	**bio+fuel**	biofuel
		$[[a]_N [b]_{Sw}]_N$	*Japan(n)+(o)logie*	**Japan+ology**	Japanese studies
Attributive	G	$[[a]_{Adj} [b]_N]_N$	*blou+draad*	**blue+wire**	galvanised wire
		$[[a]_{Num} [b]_N]_N$	*tien+kamp*	**ten+camp**	decathlon
		$[[a]_{Adv} [b]_N]_N$	*terug+weg*	**back+way**	the way back
		$[[a]_{Adv} [b]_{Adj}]_{Adj}$	*donker+blond*	**dark+blonde**	dark blonde
		$[[a]_{Num} [b]_{Adj}]_{Adj}$	*twee+maandeliks*	**two+monthly**	bimonthly
	Ph	$[[a]_{AP} [b]_N]_N$	*los-en-vas-praatjies*	**loose-and-set-talks**	random chatting
		$[[a]_{NP} [b]_N]_N$	*kop-aan-kop-botsing*	**head-on-head-collision**	head-on collision
		$[[a]_{PP} [b]_N]_N$	*in-die-lug-vraag*	**in-the-air-question**	rhetorical question
Appositive	G	$[[a]_N [b]_N]_N$	*treffer+liedjie*	**hit+song**	hit song
		$[[a]_N [b]_{Adj}]_{Adj}$	*yster+sterk*	**iron+strong**	strong as iron
		$[[a]_V [b]_{Adj}]_{Adj}$	*spring+lewendig*	**jump+lively**	alive and well
		$[[a]_P [b]_{Adj}]_{Adj}$	*deur+nat*	**through+wet**	soaked
	Ph	$[[a]_{VP} [b]_{Adj}]_{Adj}$	*kielie-my-maag-lekker*	**tickle-my-stomach-nice**	idem
		$[[a]_{NP} [b]_{Adj}]_{Adj}$	*sonsak-in-Ibiza-mooi*	**sunset-in-Ibiza-pretty**	idem
Coord	G	$[[a]_N [b]_N]_N$	*skrywer-boer*	**writer-farmer**	writer-farmer
		$[[a]_{Adj} [b]_{Adj}]_{Adj}$	*stom+verbaas*	**mute+surprised**	very surprised
		$[[a]_V [b]_V]_V$	*sit+lê*	**sit-lie**	sit and lie
		$[[a]_P [b]_P]_P$	*voor+op*	**before+above**	first
CC	Ph	$[[[a]_{Adj} [b]_N]_{NP} [c]_N]_N$	*sosiale+sekerheid(s)+reg*	**social+security+law**	social security law
		$[[[a]_{Num} [b]_N]_{NP} [c]_N]_N$	*twee+sitplek+motor*	**two+seat+car**	two-seater
		$[[[a]_P [b]_N]_{PP} [c]_N]_N$	*buite+boord+motor*	**out+board+motor**	outboard motor
SCV	G	$[[a]_P [b]_V]_V$	*in+gooi*	**in+throw**	throw in
		$[[a]_{Adv} [b]_V]_V$	*neer+gooi*	**down+throw**	throw down
		$[[a]_N [b]_V]_V$	*vleis+braai*	**meat+roast**	barbeque
Para Synth	Ph	$[[a]_{PP} extN]_N$	*ter+aarde+bestel(l)-ing*	**to+earth+deliver-extN**	burial
		$[[a]_{NP} extN]_N$	*groot+skaal-s*	**large+scale-extAdj**	large-scale
		$[[a]_{VP} extN]_N$	*alleen+lo(o)p-er*	**alone+walk-extN**	loner
	G	$[[a]_{Adj} [b]_N extAdj]_{Adj}$	*blou+kleur-ig*	**blue+colour-extAdj**	blue-coloured
		$[[a]_{Num} [b]_N extAdj]_{Adj}$	*een+bla(a)r-ig*	**one+leaf-extAdj**	monopetalous

Table 2. Prototypical endocentric compounds in Afrikaans and Dutch (with Afrikaans examples)[6]

[6] Abbreviations: VerbNex=verbal-nexus; G=ground; Ph=phrasal; NeoC=(neo-)classical; Coord=coordinate; CC=compounding compound; SCV=separable complex verb; ParaSynt=parasynthetic

Electrophysiological correlates of noun-noun compound processing by non-native speakers of English

Cecile De Cat [1], **Ekaterini Klepousniotou** [2], **Harald Baayen** [3]
[1] Linguistics & Phonetics, University of Leeds, UK
c.decat@leeds.ac.uk
[2] Institute for Psychological Sciences, University of Leeds, UK
e.klepousniotou@leeds.ac.uk
[3] Quantitative Linguistics, University of Tübingen, Germany
harald.baayen@uni-tuebingen.de

Abstract

We report on an experimental study of the processing of noun-noun compounds by native and non-native speakers of English, based on Event-Related Potentials recorded during a mask-primed lexical decision task. Analysis was by generalised linear mixed-effect modelling and generalised additive mixed modelling. Non-native processing is found to display headedness effects induced by the mothertongue. The frequency of the constituent nouns and of the intended compounds are also shown to have an effect on processing.

1 Introduction

This study examines the processing of noun-noun compounds by native and non-native speakers of English. Compounds have been extensively studied in the past 40 years from a myriad of viewpoints (Libben and Jarema, 2006; Lieber and Štekauer, 2009). A key concern has been whether the processing of compounds consists in retrieving entities listed in the mind (Butterworth, 1983) or requires decomposition into constituents listed separately (Semenza et al., 1997; Libben, 1998). Dual-routes theories contend that the two processes exist side by side (Sandra, 1990). It is now widely accepted that both constituents are activated during processing, at least in non-lexicalised compounds (Jarema, 2006; Zhang et al., 2012). Noun-noun compounds have also been shown to be processed differently to non-compounds of similar morphological complexity and length, with compounds yielding longer reaction times and different electrophysiological correlates (El Yagoubi et al., 2008).
Endocentric compounds contain a head element (*dust* in (1)) whose lexical category and interpretive features are inherited by the compound and contribute the core of its meaning (e.g. a kind of dust). The other element acts as a modifier of that head.

(1) moon dust ('dust from the moon /dust made of moon /dust with moon-like properties')

Here we focus on endocentric noun-noun compounds (henceforth NNCs), which have been argued to embody an underlying structure (Libben, 2006) that is hierarchical, involving the (possibly recursive) subordination of a modifier to a grammatical head (or a modifier-head compound, as in (2)), with head-directionality that mirrors that of other noun-complement structures in the same language (Zipser, 2013).

(2) [child [amateur [puppet <u>theatre</u>]]]

Proceedings of the First Workshop on Computational Approaches to Compound Analysis, pages 41–52, Dublin, Ireland, August 24 2014.

Headedness plays a specific role in the processing of NNCs, as demonstrated by research on Italian (which crucially features the two word orders in NNCs). Based on a lexical decision task, El Yagoubi et al. (2008) found priming effects induced by the head, independently of its position in the NNC. Headedeness effects are not distinguishable from position-in-the-string effects in languages such as English. For instance, Jarema et al. (1999) observed no difference in the priming of NNCs by the head or the modifier. Here we take this line of research further, by investigating whether headedness in the mothertongue affects the processing of transparent, irreversible NNCs in highly advanced second language learners of English.

Event-related potentials (ERPs) can provide insight into the neural activity associated with the processing of compounds. Functional interpretations can be inferred from the temporal and spatial characteristics of electromagnetic activity, and ERP components can sometimes reveal the engagement of the cognitive processes involved. Our approach is this paper is exploratory (Otten and Rugg, 2005) and will focus on identifying differences in the amplitude of the EEG signal that can be traced back to properties of the participants (such as their language background) and properties of the compounds (such as their frequency of occurrence, and the frequencies of occurrence of their constituents). Inferences based on previously identified ERP components will be drawn in the discussion as appropriate. Our research questions are: (i) Does non-native processing of NNCs result in different ERP signatures to native processing? (ii) Is non-native processing of NNCs affected by headedness effects from the mothertongue?

2 Materials and methods

We registered the electrophysiological response of the brain to visual stimuli presented in the context of a (masked) primed lexical decision task. Stimuli were irreversible NNCs presented in licit (3-a) and reversed order (3-b).

(3) a. coal dust
    b. #dust coal

The participant groups differed in mothertongue: English (control group), Spanish or German (experimental groups). Like English, German features productive compounding, with a head-last structure. Whereas in Spanish, compounds are essentially head-first, and not productive.

2.1 Participants

Ten native British English speakers (4 female, mean age 22;11 years; STD 3;3 years), ten native German learners of English (7 female, mean age 26;5 years; STD 5;7 years) and ten native Spanish learners of English (3 female, mean age 26;11 years; STD 5;3 years) took part in the study. Participants all had initial second-language exposure after 8 years of age, and all scored above 60% on a cloze test from the Cambridge Certificate in Advanced English. All were right-handed based on the Briggs and Nebes inventory (Briggs and Nebes, 1975), had no speech or language difficulties and had normal or corrected-to normal vision.

2.2 Stimuli

Experimental stimuli consisted of prime-target pairs, presented in 4 experimental conditions in a 3 (Group) x 2 (Prime Condition) x 2 (Word Order) design. The prime was either the head (e.g. *dust* in (3)) or the modifier (e.g. *coal* in (3)) of the intended compound.

The Word Order factor had 2 levels: licit (modifier - head, as in (3-a)) or reversed (head - modifier, as in (3-b)). All the NNCs were endocentric and featured a transparent, modification relationship. All items were tested for irreversibility on an independent group of 30 native speakers. The frequency of the licit compounds and their constituent nouns was estimated from the post-1990 data in Google N-grams. To avoid lexicalisation effects, only compounds with very low frequencies were included (i.e. below 3,300 — mean = 359.5, compared with a mean of 279,300 for the constituent nouns).

There was a total of 480 test items (based on 120 compounds), of which 240 are included in the present study (as we focus on the Head Prime condition only). The items were pseudo-randomised into 8 different orders (assigned randomly to participants) and presented in 4 blocks, with a rest in between.

2.3 Procedure

Participants were tested individually in a single session lasting approximately 1.5 hours. Stimuli were presented visually in light grey text on a black background. Each trial began with the visual presentation of a series of exclamation marks (!!!) for 1000 ms, which was a signal for the participant to rest their eyes and blink After a delay of 100 ms a fixation point (+) was presented for 250 ms to signal that the trial was about to begin. After a 100 ms mask (#######), the prime was presented for 100 ms followed by a second mask (for 50 ms) and the target (for 1000 ms). After a delay of 500 ms a question mark (?) appeared for 2000 ms during which time participants had to make a lexical decision about the target (as acceptable or not) by pressing (with their right hand) one of two buttons on a hand-held button box (counterbalanced across participants). Participants were instructed to respond as accurately as possible; accuracy and reaction times (in ms from the onset of the "?") were recorded. After the response (or at the end of 2000 ms if the participant did not respond), there was a delay of 100 ms before the next trial started. The experimental session was preceded by a practice session comprising 20 trials, which was repeated until participants could perform the task and procedure with no errors (usually one or two practice sessions sufficed).

The EEG was recorded (Neuroscan Synamps2) from 60 Ag/AgCl electrodes embedded in a cap based on the extended version of the International 10-20 positioning system (Sharbrough et al., 1991). Additional electrodes were placed on the left and right mastoids. Data were recorded using a central reference electrode placed between Cz and CPz. The ground electrode was positioned between Fz and Fpz. To capture noise articfacts in the EEG signal due to eye movements, electro-oculograms (EOGs) were recorded using electrodes positioned at either side of the eyes, and above and below the left eye. At the beginning of the experiment electrode impedances were below 10 kΩ. The analogue EEG and EOG recordings were amplified (band pass filter 0.1 to 100Hz), and continuously digitised (32-bit) at a sampling frequency of 500 Hz. Data were processed offline using Neuroscan Edit 4.3 software (Compumedics Neuroscan) and filtered (0.1-40Hz, 96 dB/Oct, Butterworth zero phase filter). The effect of eye-blink artifacts was minimised by estimating and correcting their contribution to the EEG using a regression procedure which involves calculating an average blink from 32 blinks for each participant, and removing the contribution of the blink from all other channels on a point-by-point basis. Data were epoched between -100 and 1100 ms relative to the onset of the experimental targets and baseline-corrected by subtracting the mean amplitude over the pre-stimulus interval. Epochs were rejected if participants did not make a response within the allocated time (during presentation of the "?"), or if they made an incorrect response. Subsequently the data was downsampled to 125 Hz. Trial rejection was not done *a priori* but based on the residuals of the modelling, resulting in only 0.7% of discarded data.

3 Results

3.1 Accuracy analysis

The responses on the lexical decision task were analysed with a generalised linear mixed-effect model with a binomial link function, using the `lme4` package, version 1.0-4 (Bates et al., 2013) with the 'bobyqa' optimizer. Only those predictors that contributed to the model fit were retained, as shown in Table 1. The covariate 'Compound Frequency' did not reach significance. The model provided a substantially improved fit compared to the null-hypothesis model with random intercepts for participant and item only.

	Coefficient	Std. Error	Z	p
Intercept	-0.7565	1.7174	-0.4405	0.6596
Word Order: Licit	-0.0828	0.1644	-0.5035	0.6146
L1: German	-0.6339	0.3123	-2.0299	0.0424
L1: Spanish	-0.7670	0.4135	-1.8549	0.0636
Proficiency	3.7191	1.7052	2.1811	0.0292
Word Order: Licit by L1: German	0.8710	0.1474	5.9074	0.0000
Word Order: Licit by L1: Spanish	0.9322	0.1410	6.6101	0.0000

Table 1: Coefficients of a logistic mixed-effects regression model fitted to the accuracy data. The reference level for Word Order is Reversed, and for L1: English

Table 1 indicates that for English speakers, accuracy did not differ for the licit and reversed word order conditions. For non-native speakers, accuracy was higher in the Licit Word Order condition, compared with the Reversed Word Order condition. Across groups, greater proficiency afforded higher accuracy. Figure 1 visualizes this pattern of results.

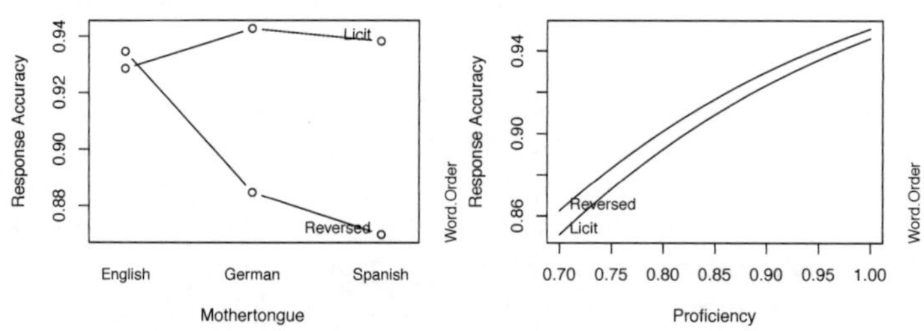

Figure 1: Partial effects of the predictors in the logistic model for response accuracy.

3.2 ERP analysis

We analysed the electrophysiological response elicited by the presentation of compound words with the generalized additive mixed model (GAMM, (Wood, 2006; Tremblay and Baayen, 2010; Baayen, to appear; Baayen et al., in preparation; Kryuchkova et al., 2012)). Generalized additive mixed models extend the generalized linear mixed model with tools (thin plate regression splines, tensor product smooths) for modeling *non-linear* functional relations between one or more predictors and a response variable. GAMMs, as implemented in the mgcv package 1.7-28, offer three important advantages for the analysis of EEG data compared to standard linear models and analysis of variance. First, GAMMs are optimized for dealing with non-linear functional relations between a response (here, the amplitude) and one or more numerical predictors (resulting in wiggly curves, wiggly surfaces, or, in the case of more than two predictors, wiggly hypersurfaces). Second, GAMMs decompose the EEG amplitude into a sequence of additive components, thereby affording the analyst a toolkit for separating out partial effects due to different kinds of predictors (e.g., language group, time, compound frequency, constituent frequency). Third, GAMMs can capture AR1 autocorrelative processes in the signal, and therefore protect against anti-conservative p-values and mistakingly taking noise for complex EPR signatures (as has been shown to occur by Tanner et al., 2013).

We include for analysis only trials that elicited a correct response. The time window analysed was limited to 0–800 ms, time-locked to the onset of stimulus presentation. Autocorrelations in the residual error were removed by including in the GAMM an autocorrelation parameter $\rho = 0.9$ for AR1 error for each basic time series in the data (the time series amplitudes for each unique combination of subject and item). Inclusion of ρ was essential for removing most of the autocorrelational structure from the model's residuals.

A. parametric coefficients	Estimate	Std. Error	t-value	p-value
Intercept (English Reversed)	-0.6815	1.8695	-0.3645	0.7155
Compound Frequency (English Reversed)	0.0659	0.0756	0.8711	0.3837
English:Licit	1.0720	0.1845	5.8103	< 0.0001
German:Reversed	0.6172	2.5967	0.2377	0.8121
German:Licit	0.8199	2.5977	0.3156	0.7523
Spanish:Reversed	0.0311	2.5986	0.0120	0.9905
Spanish:Licit	-3.6624	2.6002	-1.4085	0.1590
Comp. Frequency:English Licit	-0.2747	0.0392	-7.0097	< 0.0001
Comp. Frequency:German Reversed	-0.0577	0.0405	-1.4254	0.1540
Comp. Frequency:German Licit	-0.0826	0.0397	-2.0837	0.0372
Comp. Frequency:Spanish Reversed	-0.1139	0.0414	-2.7536	0.0059
Comp. Frequency:Spanish Licit	0.2361	0.0404	5.8473	< 0.0001
B. smooth terms	edf	Ref.df	F-value	p-value
smooth in Time English:Licit	8.5809	8.7860	11.5648	< 0.0001
diff. curve Time: German:Licit	1.0111	1.0212	0.1285	0.7255
diff. curve Time: Spanish:Licit	6.7504	7.8925	4.4964	< 0.0001
diff. curve Time: English:Reversed	1.9025	2.3906	1.0696	0.3436
diff. curve Time: German:Reversed	1.0074	1.0141	0.4174	0.5210
diff. curve Time: Spanish:Reversed	1.0069	1.0095	1.6952	0.1925
tensor product surface F1 and F2 (English, Licit)	3.0189	3.0349	2.1154	0.0951
diff. surface German:Licit	11.2569	12.3579	7.2697	< 0.0001
diff. surface Spanish:Licit	12.9312	13.6137	60.1585	< 0.0001
diff. surface English:Reversed	3.9839	4.0083	17.6082	< 0.0001
diff. surface German:Reversed	9.0655	10.4566	5.5875	< 0.0001
diff. surface Spanish:Reversed	14.7736	14.9639	28.2189	< 0.0001
random intercepts Compound	107.6142	111.0000	34.7869	< 0.0001
by-subject random wiggly curves Trial	163.4484	267.0000	43.8796	< 0.0001
by-subject random wiggly curves Time	170.5793	267.0000	2.4442	< 0.0001

Table 2: Generalized additive mixed model fitted to the amplitude of the electrophysiological response of the brain to English compounds at channel C1.

In what follows, we focus on channel C1, which revealed a pattern of results typical for surrounding channels. The amplitude of the EEG signal was modeled (without any prior averaging) as an additive function of Word order (Licit vs. Reversed), Compound Frequency, the Constituent Frequency of Modifier and of Head, and Participant Group (English, German, Spanish). Proficiency did not reach significance and did not improve the model fit significantly, so we did not include this predictor in the final model.

GAMMs currently can only accomodate interactions of smooths with a single factor. In order to study the interaction of speaker group and word order, we therefore created a new factor GO with

as levels English:Licit, English:Reversed, German:Licit, German:Reversed, Spanish:Licit, and Spanish:Reversed, using treatment contrasts with as reference level English:Reversed. In the parametric part of the model (the upper half of Table 2), the coefficients for the main effect of GO and its interaction with compound frequency are to be interpreted in the familiar way, with the interaction terms specifying differences in the slope of compound frequency for the non-reference levels of GO.
GO also interacted with the constituent frequencies. For this three-way interaction, we recoded GO as an ordered factor, which is how the `bam` function of the MGCV package is instructed to construct a reference surface (in our implementation, for English:Licit) and difference surfaces for the other factor levels with respect to the standard compound forms as read by English native speakers.
Table 2 summarizes the GAMM fitted to the amplitude of the EEG signal at channel C1. First consider the parametric part of the model, presented in the upper half of the table, which concerns the main effect of GO and its interaction with log-transformed compound frequency. This interaction is summarized in Figure 2. Black lines denote the Licit Word Order condition, grey lines the Reversed Word Order condition. Compound frequency did not have much of an effect in the Reversed conditions.

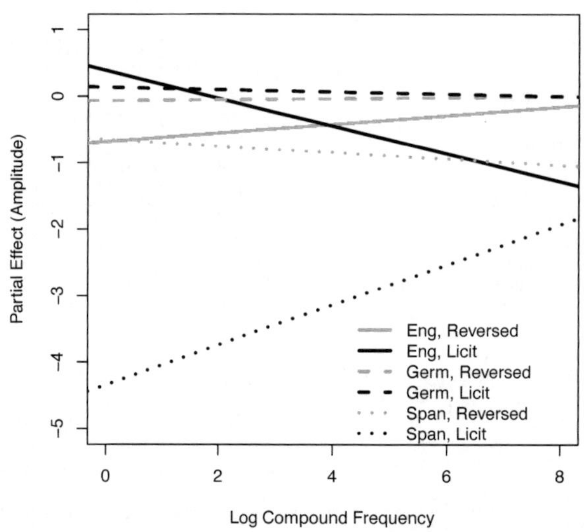

Figure 2: The three-way interaction of Participant Group, Grammaticality, and Compound Frequency.

For English (solid lines), a compound frequency is present in the licit condition, with greater compound frequencies inducing more negative amplitudes. For German (dashed lines), the slope was close to zero in both conditions, indicating the absence of a frequency effect. The Spanish speakers (dotted lines) revealed a regression line with an opposite slope to that for the English speakers in the Licit condition, and with a much lower intercept. This reversal of the slope, as compared to English, may be a consequence of the fact that in Spanish, translation equivalents would be expressed with the opposite constituent order.
The non-parametric part of the model, reported in the lower half of Table 2, handles non-linear effects in the model, using thin plate regression splines for wiggly curves and tensor product smooths for wiggly surfaces. The first row of the non-parametric subtable summarizes a smooth in time for English

licit compounds. This smooth is visualized in the left panel of Figure 3, together with its 95% confidence interval. The model required 8.78 effective degrees of freedom (edf) to capture a (significant) positive inflection around 300 ms post stimulus onset. (Higher edfs indicate greater wiggliness.) The next 5 rows in Table 2 describe the difference curves for the remaining levels of GO. The only level for which this difference curve is significant is Spanish:Licit. The second panel of Figure 3 presents this difference curve, which required 7.89 effective degrees of freedom. As the difference curve is significantly above the X-axis around 300 ms post stimulus onset, and significantly below the X-axis after 600 ms, we conclude that the Spanish speakers reading licit compounds had a higher positivity around 300 ms compared to the English speakers reading the same compound, combined with more negative amplitudes after 600 ms post stimulus.

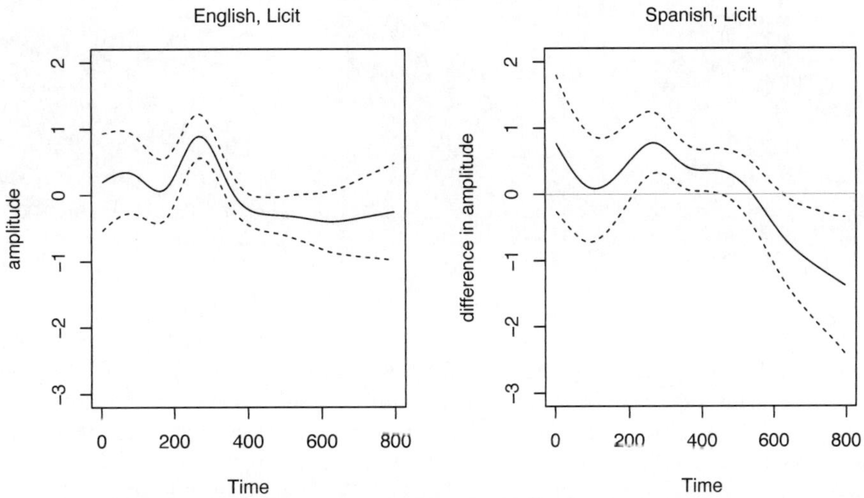

Figure 3: The interaction of participant Group, Grammaticality, and Time. The left panel shows the smooth for English in the Licit Word Order condition; the right panel shows the difference curve with respect to the left panel for the Spanish participants.

EEG amplitudes were also modulated by an interaction of the constituent frequencies by GO, which we modeled with a tensor surface for English:Licit and difference tensor surfaces for the other levels of GO. The second set of 6 rows in Table 2 present the summary statistics, and Figure 3 the smoothed surfaces. The upper left panel presents the reference smooth for English native speakers reading compounds in their licit order. For channel C1, this surface is not well-supported statistically ($p = 0.095$), but at neighboring channels (e.g., Cz, FC1) higher-frequency constituents elicited significantly higher amplitudes. Interestingly, when the constituents are reversed, significantly more negative amplitudes for compounds with high constituent frequencies are observed for native English speakers, as shown in the lower left panel. German speakers show a similar pattern with more negative amplitudes for both licit and reversed compounds (center panels). The strongest negativities are present for Spanish speakers in the licit condition (upper right). In the reversed condition, Spanish speakers show a pattern of somewhat increased negativity (lower right) that, however, does not vary much with constituent frequency.

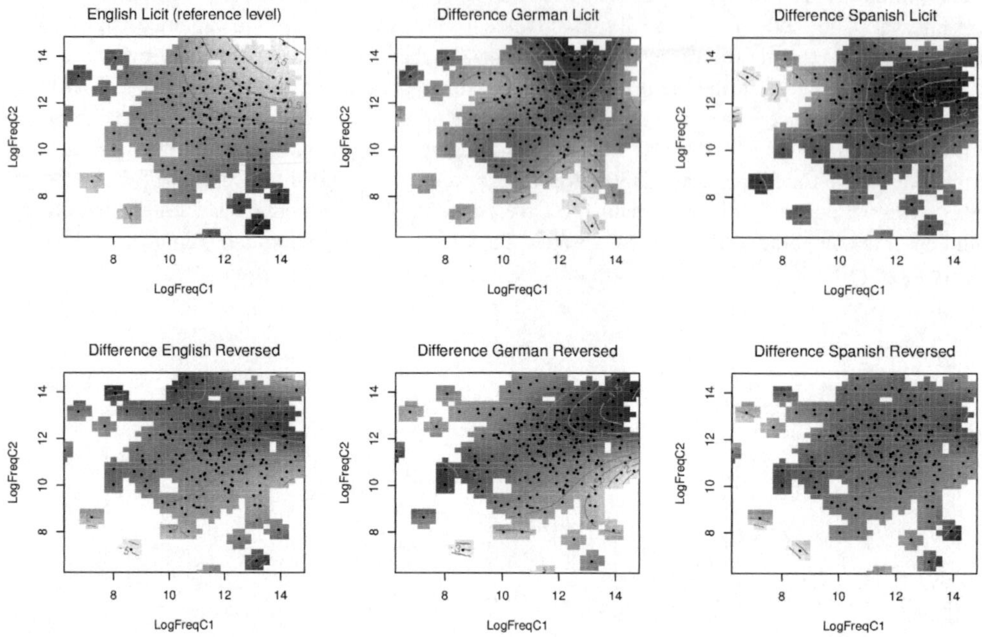

Figure 4: The interaction of left and right constituent frequency by grammaticality and language group. The upper left panel presents the smooth surface for English:Licit, the remaining panels present difference surfaces with respect to the English:Licit condition. Darker shades of gray indicate more negative amplitudes. Contour lines are 0.5 units apart in panels 1, 2, 5, and 6; they are 2 units apart in panel 3, and 1 unit apart in panel 4.

The final three rows of Table 2 specify the random-effects structure of the model. Random intercepts for compound were included in order to allow for differences in baseline amplitude across compounds. For subjects, two random wiggly curves were included. The first models changes in amplitude as subjects go through the experiment. The second models subject-specific changes over within-trial time. The random wiggly curves are the nonlinear equivalent of what in the context of a linear mixed-effects model would be 'random straight lines' obtained by combining random intercepts with random slopes. For EEG data, where amplitude changes non-linearly with time, the flexibility of penalized and shrunk regression splines is essential.

4 Discussion

The non-native participants performed the lexical decision task with a high level of accuracy. For the licit compounds, accuracy was comparable to that of native speakers. For reversed compounds, accuracy dropped slightly, from around 94% to around 88%. From this, we conclude, first, that all subjects have acquired NNC structures in English, and second, that non-native speakers are more likely to accept novel noun combinations as English compounds.

Knowledge of whether a two-word combination is in fact licit in English can arise from two sources. On the one hand, speakers may be familiar with the compound, as evidenced by an effect of compound frequency. For the native English speakers resonding to licit compounds, an effect of compound frequency was indeed present in the EEG amplitudes. On the other hand, speakers may infer the intended meaning from the constituents (e.g., English *beach ball* indexing German *Wasserball*, 'water ball'). Constituent effects were well attested in the EEG amplitudes. Interestingly, for English speakers, constituent frequency effects gave rise to more positive amplitudes in the licit condition (significantly at neighboring channels) whereas in the reversed condition, amplitudes were more negative for higher-frequency constituents. In other words, when English speakers are confronted with reversed compounds, which for them are actually novel compounds, the compound frequency effect disappears, and a constituent frequency effect emerges that is opposite in sign to that for normal compounds.

Of the non-native speakers of English, only the Spanish speakers revealed a compound frequency effect, with a slope opposite in sign to that for the English speakers. If higher amplitude in the signal indicates increased processing effort, the effect of the frequency of the intended compound could be interpreted as facilitating in the Licit Word Order condition in the native speakers but inhibiting in the Spanish group (and without much effect in the German group). We hypothesize that Spanish speakers find licit English compounds more difficult precisely because in their native language, the order of the constituents would have been reversed. It is only these speakers that have a word order conflict to resolve.

All speakers (non-native as well as English) responding to reversed (i.e., for them, novel) compounds, show more negative amplitudes for compounds with higher constituent frequencies. We interpret this as evidence for constituent-driven, decompositional processing. The especially pronounced negativities for Spanish speakers in the Licit Word Order context (which go hand in hand with a positive slope for compound frequency) suggest that for these speakers increased processing resources are called upon to resolve the conflict between English and Spanish constituent order, in spite of native-like performance in the evaluation of compounds in that condition.

A positive peak around 300 ms post-stimulus was found in all groups in both conditions, and exacerbated in the Spanish group in the Licit Word Order condition. This peak could be interpreted as a P300, indexing attentional resources. El Yagoubi et al. (2008) found that right-headed NNCs in Italian yielded a greater P300 and interpreted this as evidence that processing this marked (but in Italian equally grammatical) word order required increased attentional resources. If the P300 observed here reflects a peak of attentional engagement, we expect its amplitude to predict scores on an Attention Network Task (Fan et al., 2005) — something we will investigate in the next phase of this study.

With respect to the absence of a significant N400 effect between the Word Order conditions, we first note that the N400 may vanish due to familiarization, and also to masked priming (Coulson et al., 2005; Brown and Hagoort, 1993). However, and perhaps more importantly, reversed compounds are not semantically anomalous. To the contrary, they invite interpretation and, as we have documented, give rise to constituent-driven processes of interpretation. From this perspective, an N400 would then characterize the processing of semantic anomalies that cannot be resolved through morphological processing.

5 Concluding remarks

This study set out to investigate (i) whether non-native processing of NNCs results in different ERP signatures compared to native processing, and (ii) whether non-native processing of NNCs is affected by constituent order in the mothertongue. Analysis of the EEG amplitudes revealed that English native speakers read licit compounds using both whole-word information (as indexed by compound frequency) in congruence with constituent information (as indexed by constituent frequency with a positive effect) whereas non-native speakers and English speakers reading novel (reversed) compounds resort to decompositional interpretation indexed by a negative effect on amplitudes. Further-

more, Spanish readers undergo interference from the different constituent order possibilities in their own language, leading to a reversed compound frequency effect and strongly enhanced constituent frequency effects (with a negative sign) when reading English licit compounds.
This pattern of results is, for native speakers, consistent with the early effects of compound frequency observed using eye-tracking by, e.g., Kuperman et al. (2008, 2009) and Miwa et al. (2014) for English, Finnish, and Japanese respectively. The importance of constituent-driven processing for non-native speakers is reminiscent of the decompositional eye-movement patterns of less-proficient readers reported by Kuperman & Van Dyke (2011).
We conclude with noting that the insights gleaned from the EEG amplitudes would not have been possible without generalized additive mixed models. At the same time, we believe we are only seeing the tip of the iceberg. For instance, the model can be improved by allowing the interaction of the constituent frequencies by group and constituent order to vary with time, using a five-way tensor product smooth. Two considerations have withheld us from following up on this considerably more complex model. First, without specific hypotheses as a guide, interpretation becomes extremely difficult. Second, we are concerned that with a relative small number of compounds (120), overfitting might become an issue. For future research specifically addressing the development over time of constituent (and whole-word) frequency effects, we recommend designs with larger numbers of compounds.

6 Acknowledgments

This project was financed by pump-priming funds from the University of Leeds' Faculty of Arts and by a British Academy Quantitative Skills Acquisition award (SQ120066) to the first author. Many thanks to Antoine Tremblay for help with the initial data preparation, to Cyrus Shaoul for friendly technical and coding advice, to Jacolien van Rij for helpful suggestions for the gamm analysis and to Raphael Morschett, Chris Norton, Kremena Koleva and Natasha Rust for the data collection and pre-processing.

References

R.Harald Baayen, Jacolien van Rij, Cécile De Cat, and Simon Wood. in preparation. Autocorrelated errors in experimental data in the language sciences: Some solutions offered by generalized additive mixed models.

R. Harald Baayen. to appear. *Analyzing Linguistic Data. A Practical Introduction to Statistics Using R (second, augmented edition).* CUP, Cambridge.

Douglas Bates, Martin Maechler, Ben Bolker, and Steven Walker, 2013. *lme4: Linear mixed-effects models using Eigen and S4.* R package version 1.0-4.

G.G. Briggs and R.D. Nebes. 1975. Patterns of hand preference in a student population. *Cortex*, 11:230–238.

Colin Brown and Peter Hagoort. 1993. The processing nature of the n400: Evidence from masked priming. *Journal of Cognitive Neuroscience*, 5(1):34–44.

B. Butterworth. 1983. Lexical representation. In B. Butterworth, editor, *Language Production*, pages 257–294. Academic Press, San Diego, CA.

S. Coulson, Kara D. Federmeier, C. Van Petten, and Marta Kutas. 2005. Right hemisphere sensitivity to word- and sentence-level context: Evidence from event-related brain potentials. *Journal of Experimental Psychology: Learning, Memory, & Cognition*, 31:129–147.

Radouane El Yagoubi, Valentina Chiarelli, Sara Mondini, Gelsomina Perrone, Morena Danieli, and Carlo Semenza. 2008. Neural correlates of Italian nominal compounds and potential impacts of headedness effect: An ERP study. *Cognitive Neuropsychology*, 25(4):559–581.

Jin Fan, Bruce D. McCandliss, John Fossella, Jonathan I. Flombaum, and Michael Posner. 2005. The activation of attentional networks. *NeuroImage*, 26(2):471–479.

Gonia Jarema, C. Busson, R. Nikolova, K. Tsapkini, and Gary Libben. 1999. Processing compounds: A cross-linguistic study. *Brain and Language*, 68:362–369.

Gonia Jarema. 2006. Compound representation and processing: A cross-language perspective. In Gary Libben and Gonia Jarema, editors, *The Representation and Processing of Compound Words*, pages 45–70. OUP, Oxford.

T. Kryuchkova, B. V. Tucker, L. Wurm, and R. H. Baayen. 2012. Danger and usefulness in auditory lexical processing: evidence from electroencephalography. *Brain and Language*, 122:81–91.

V. Kuperman and J.A. Van Dyke. 2011. Effects of individual differences in verbal skills on eye-movement patterns duing sentence reading. *Journal of memory and language*, 65(1):42–73.

V. Kuperman, R. Bertram, and R. H. Baayen. 2008. Morphological dynamics in compound processing. *Language and Cognitive Processes*, 23:1089–1132.

V. Kuperman, R. Schreuder, R. Bertram, and R. H. Baayen. 2009. Reading of multimorphemic Dutch compounds: Towards a multiple route model of lexical processing. *Journal of Experimental Psychology: HPP*, 35:876–895.

Gary Libben and Gonia Jarema, editors. 2006. *The Representation and Processing of Compound Words*. OUP, Oxford.

Gary Libben. 1998. Semantic transparency in the processing of compounds. *Brain and Language*, 61:30–44.

Gary Libben. 2006. Why study compound processing? An overview of the issues. In Gary Libben and Gonia Jarema, editors, *The Representation and Processing of Compound Words*, pages 1–22. OUP, Oxford.

Rochelle Lieber and Pavol Štekauer, editors. 2009. *The Oxford Handbook of Compounding*. Oxford University Press, Oxford.

Koji Miwa, Gary Libben, Ton Dijkstra, and Harald Baayen. 2014. The time-course of lexical activation in japanese morphographic word recognitin: Evidence for a character-driven processing model. *The Quarterly Journal of Experimental Psychology*, 67(1):79–113.

Leun Otten and Michael Rugg. 2005. Interpreting event-related brain potentials. In Todd Handy, editor, *Event-related potentials: A methods handbook*, pages 3–17. MIT Press, Cambridge, MA.

D. Sandra. 1990. On the representation and processing of compound words: Automatic access to constituent morphemes does not occur. *The Quarterly Journal of Experimental Psychology*, 42A:529–567.

Carlo Semenza, C. Luzzatti, and S. Carabelli. 1997. Morphological represntation of compound nouns: A study on Italian aphasic patients. *Journal of Neurolinguistics*, 10:33–43.

F. Sharbrough, G.E. Chatrian, R.P. Lesser, H. Luders, M. Nuwer, and T.W. Picton. 1991. American electroencephalographic society guidelines for standard electrode position nomenclature. *Journal of Clinical Neurophysiology*, 8:200–202.

Darren Tanner, Kayo Inoue, and Lee Osterhout. 2013. Brain-based individual differences in online L2 grammatical comprehension. *Bilingualism: Language and Cognition*, 17(2):277–293.

Antoine Tremblay and R. Harald Baayen. 2010. Holistic processing of regular four-word sequences: A behavioral and ERP study of the effects of structure, frequency, and probability on immediate free recall. In D. Wood, editor, *Perspectives on formulaic language: Acquisition and communication*, pages 151–173. The Continuum International Publishing Group., London.

Simon Wood. 2006. *Generalised additive models: An introduction with R*. Chapman and Hall/CRC, Boca Raton, FL.

J. I. E. Zhang, Richard C. Anderson, Qiuying Wang, Jerome Packard, Xinchun Wu, Shan Tang, and Xiaoling Ke. 2012. Insight into the structure of compound words among speakers of chinese and english. *Applied Psycholinguistics*, 33(4):753–779.

Katharina Zipser. 2013. Proto-language, phrase structure and nominal compounds. Which of them fit together? In *Poster presented at ICL 2013, Geneva*.

A Comparative Study of Different Classification Methods for the Identification of Brazilian Portuguese Multiword Expressions

Alexsandro Fonseca **Fatiha Sadat**

Université du Québec à Montréal, 201 av. President Kennedy,
Montreal, QC, H2X 3Y7, Canada
affonseca@gmail.com sadat.fatiha@uqam.ca

Abstract

This paper presents a comparative study of different methods for the identification of multiword expressions, applied to a Brazilian Portuguese corpus. First, we selected the candidates based on the frequency of bigrams. Second, we used the linguistic information based on the grammatical classes of the words forming the bigrams, together with the frequency information in order to compare the performance of different classification algorithms. The focus of this study is related to different classification techniques such as support-vector machines (SVM), multi-layer perceptron, naïve Bayesian nets, decision trees and random forest. Third, we evaluated three different multi-layer perceptron training functions in the task of classifying different patterns of multiword expressions. Finally, our study compared two different tools, MWEtoolkit and Text-NSP, for the extraction of multiword expression candidates using different association measures.

1 Introduction

The identification of multiword expressions (MWEs) and their appropriate handling is necessary in constructing professional tools for language manipulation (Hurskainen, 2008). MWEs are considered as a very challenging problem for various natural language processing (NLP) applications, such as machine translation.

There are several definitions of MWE in the scientific literature. Smadja (1993) defines MWE as an arbitrary and recurrent word combination; while Choueka (1988) defines them as a syntactic and semantic unit whose exact meaning or connotation cannot be derived directly and unambiguously from the meaning or connotation of its components. Moreover, Sag et al. (2002) defines MWE as an idiosyncratic interpretation that exceeds the limit of the word (or spaces).

We adopt in this paper a definition similar to the one given by Sag et al. (2002): a MWE is an expression formed by two or more words, whose meaning can vary from totally dependent to completely independent of the meaning of its constituent words. Examples of MWEs: "take care", "Bill Gates", "coffee break" and "by the way".

This study treats only two-word MWEs. We are not considering some common Portuguese MWEs, such as "tempo de espera" (waiting time, lit.: time of waiting), "dar um tempo" (to have a break, lit.: to give a time) or "começar tudo de novo" (restart, lit. start everything of new). However, our experience and some related work show that we are already covering the majority of MWEs. For their data, for example, Piao et al. (2003, Section 5) found that 81.88% of the recognized MWEs were bigrams. Moreover, our focus is in MWE formed by nouns, adjectives, verbs and adverbs. As a consequence, two-word MWEs formed by prepositions were not considered, such as "de novo" (again, lit. of new), "à toa" (for nothing), "apesar de" (despite of) or "desde ontem" (since yesterday). In resume, we evaluated the performance of different classification algorithms and tools for the recognition of two-word MWEs formed by nouns, adjectives, verbs and adverbs. We intend, in the future, to extend this study to MWEs formed by words belonging to any grammatical class and having any number of words.

Proceedings of the First Workshop on Computational Approaches to Compound Analysis, pages 53–62, Dublin, Ireland, August 24 2014.

The correct identification of MWEs is important for different NLP applications, such as machine translation, information retrieval and the semantic web, to which the principle of syntactic or semantic unit is important (Watrin and François, 2011).

Methods for identifying MWEs rely on statistical measures, especially association measures, such as mutual information (Church and Hanks, 1990), log-likelihood or Dice's coefficient (Smadja, 1996).

The basic idea behind such measures can be summarized as follows: the higher the association among the words that appear together in a text, the higher the probability that they constitute a single semantic unit.

There are other methods, which use linguistic information or hybrid approaches that combine statistical measures with the linguistic information, such as the grammatical class of each word, the sense of the composite expression or the syntactic regularities.

2 Related Work

Dias and Lopes (2005) present a method for the extraction of MWEs based only on statistics with an application on the Portuguese language. This method consists of a new association measure called "mutual expectation". Their method can be applied to extract MWEs formed by two or more words, contiguous or not. The mutual expectation method is based on the LocalMaxs (Silva and Lopes, 1999) algorithm. This algorithm deduces that a n-gram is a MWE if the degree of attraction between its words is greater or equal to the degree of attraction of all its subsets of n-1 words (i.e. all groups of n-1 words contained by the n-gram) and if it is strictly greater than the degree of attraction of all of its super groups of n+1 words (i.e. all groups of n+1 words containing the n-gram). When the n-gram is a bigram (n = 2), only the degree of attraction of its super groups of n+1 words is calculated.

Ramisch et al. (2008) analyze the extraction of MWEs based only on statistical information, comparing three association measures: the mutual information, chi-squared and permutation entropy. Then they introduce a method called entropy of permutation and insertion (a hybrid approach), that takes into account linguistic information of the MWE type. Following some patterns, they modify each original MWE candidate by inserting some types of words in some positions and they test if the new MWE are still MWE and they try to identify which kind of modification an MWE type accepts or refuses in a particular language. The new measure is calculated using a formula that combines the probability of occurrence of the original and of the generated MWE.

Agarwal et al. (2004) present an approach for extracting MWEs in languages with few resources based on a morphological analyser and a moderate size untagged text corpus. First, they divide the MWEs in categories. For example, Category-2 is formed by noun-noun, adjective-noun and verb-verb bigrams. Then they apply a set of rules to identify or eliminate candidates as MWE. Those rules take into consideration the precedent and/or the next word in the pair and the possible inflections of the words. After this step, association measures are computed.

Piao et al. (2003) use, what they call, a semantic field annotator. They use a semantic tagger for the English language called USAS, developed in Lancaster University. This tagger labels words and expressions in a text using 21 categories. For example, Category-A is used for "general and abstract terms", Category-B is used for "the body and the individual", Category-E is used for "emotion", etc. A text labeled with those categories is used to extract the MWE candidates. The differential of this approach is that the candidates are selected not based only on statistical measures. The problem with this is that most of the MWEs, about 68% in the work of Piao et al., appear in the text with a low frequency. As a consequence, most of the methods for extracting MWEs give good precision, but low recall.

3 The Data

The current study used the corpus CETENFolha (Corpus de Extractos de Textos Eletrónicos NILC/Folha de São Paulo), available on the website Linguateca Portuguesa (CETENFolha, 2008). This corpus is composed by excerpts from Brazilian newspaper "Folha de São Paulo", and contains over 24 million words. It is part of a project on the automatic processing of the Portuguese (Kinoshita et al., 2006). As the current stage, we used a small fraction of the corpus, composed by 3,409 excerpts of text (about 250,000 words). Each excerpt corresponds to individual news, which covers different areas.

4 Comparison of different classification algorithms

4.1 Pre-processing the data

Before the indexation, some pre-processing methods on the corpus were completed, such as lemmatization and elimination of stop words (articles, prepositions, conjunctions). In this study, we are mostly interested in analyzing MWEs formed by nouns, adjectives, adverbs and verbs. And since those stop words are very common in Portuguese, their elimination reduces considerably the number of MWE candidates that would not be relevant to this study.

We created two indexes: one formed only of bigrams and the other only by unigrams. Our results show 49,589 bigrams, with 1,170 having a frequency higher than 3. We selected those 1,170 bigrams as our MWE candidates. By hand, from the 1,170 candidates, we recognized 447 as being Portuguese MWEs.

The main criterion used to consider a bigram as a MWE was that the bigram had a sense on its own. For example: proper names, like "Adelson Barbosa", "George Bush" and "Belo Horizonte"; support verb constructions: "tomar cuidado" (to take care), "fazer sentido" (to make sense); expressions having some idiomatic sense: "abrir mão" (to give up, lit. to open hand), "fazer questão" (to insist, to require [that something be done in a specific way], lit. to make question); fixed expressions: "bens duráveis" (durable goods), "senso comum" (common sense), "curto prazo" (short term). Example of bigrams not considered as MWE: "Brasil foi" (Brazil was), "apenas dois" (only two), "bomba matou" (bomb killed), etc.

For each bigram, we found the frequency of its constituent words in the unigram index. Then, we classified by hand each of the words by their grammatical class: 1 for nouns, 2 for adjectives, 3 for verbs, 4 for other classes (mostly adverbs and pronouns) and 5 for proper names. This gave us 25 patterns of bigrams: N-N, N-ADJ, N-V, V-N, PN-PN, etc. We decided not to use a POS-tagger, to ensure that each word would have its grammatical class assigned correctly, creating the most correct possible training and testing data sets for the classification algorithms.

We then created a matrix of 1,170 lines and five columns. For each line, the first column represents the frequency of a bigram in the excerpt of text, the second column represents the frequency of the first bigram's word, the third column represents the frequency of the second bigram's word, the fourth column represents the grammatical class of the first bigram's word and the fifth column represents the grammatical class of the second bigram's word. This matrix was used to evaluate the precision and recall of different classification algorithms.

4.2 Evaluation

We applied nine different classification algorithms to our data set. The parameters used with each algorithm are listed below.

Decision tree: C4.5 algorithm (Quinlan, 1993) with confidence factor = 0.25.

Random Forest (Breiman, 2001): number of trees = 10; max depth = 0; seed = 1.

Ada Boost (Freund and Schapire, 1996): classifier = decision stamp; weight threshold = 100; iterations = 10; seed = 1.

Bagging (Breiman, 1996): classifier = fast decision tree learner (min. number = 2; min. variance = 0.001; number of folds = 3; seed = 1; max. depth = -1); bag size percent = 100; seed = 1; number of execution slots = 1; iterations = 10.

KNN (Aha and Kibler, 1991): K = 3; window size = 0; search algorithm = linear NN search (distance function = Euclidian distance).

SVM (Chang and Lin, 2001): cache size = 40; cost = 1; degree = 3; eps = 0.001; loss = 0.1; kernel type = radial basis function; nu = 0.5; seed = 1.

Multilayer perceptron: learning rate = 0.3; momentum = 0.2; training time = 500; validation threshold = 500; seed = 0;

Bayesian net: search algorithm = k2 (Cooper and Herskovits, 1992); estimator = simple estimator (alpha = 0.5).

As we can see in Table 1, the values of precision are very similar for all the algorithms, varying between 0.830 (random forest) and 0.857 (bagging), with the exception of SVM, which gave a precision of 0.738. The recall values were between 0.831 and 0.857 (0.655 for SVM).

We obtained good precision and recall. However, we must consider that the values of recall are based only on the MWEs present in our reference list, and not in the entire corpus, since we could not count all the MWEs present in the corpus.

Algorithm	TP Rate	FP Rate	Precision	Recall
Decision tree	0.853	0.158	0.854	0.853
Random forest	0.831	0.194	0.830	0.831
Ada boost	0.837	0.196	0.836	0.837
Bagging	0.857	0.163	0.857	0.857
KNN – k = 3	0.846	0.171	0.846	0.846
SVM	0.655	0.553	0.738	0.655
M. perceptron	0.852	0.174	0.851	0.852
Naïve B. net	0.836	0.170	0.839	0.836
Bayesian net	0.842	0.170	0.843	0.842

Table 1: True-positive rate, false-positive rate, precision and recall for nine classification algorithms.

5 Bigrams patterns classification

We chose one of the algorithms with the best performance (multi-layer perceptron) and we evaluated it using three different training functions, bayesian regulation back propagation (br), Levenberg-Marquardt (lm) and scaled conjugate gradient (scg), and compared their performance in the classification of different patterns of bigrams as MWE. For this comparison we used the patterns that gave 10 or more samples of MWEs. We had eight patterns that together represent 59% of the candidate bigrams (689/1,170) and 94% of the MWEs that appear three or more times in the corpus (420/447). The tables 2.a, 2.b and 2.c show the results. "N" stands for "Noun", "A" for adjective, "O" for other classes (mostly adverbs and pronouns) and "PN" for "proper names".

Analyzing the three tables, we see that we had best results with the patterns N-A (e.g. "agencias internacionais", "ajuste fiscal", "America Latina") and PN-PN ("Adelson Barbosa", "Ayrton Senna", "Bill Clinton"). The function lm gave the best value for the F1 measure (0.912) for the pattern N-A, and the function scg gave the best value for the pattern PN-PN (0.931).

In general, we obtained the weakest results with the patterns O-N (e.g. ex-presidente, primeiro mundo) and A-PN (São Paulo, Nova York). Using the training functions "lm" and "scg", none of the 10 MWEs belonging to the pattern O-O (apesar disso, além disso) was recognized, and none of the 46 MWEs belonging to the pattern O-N was recognized, when using the training function "scg".

The last line of each table show the total values for the eight patterns, for the three learning functions. We had the best precision and recall using the "lm" function.

Pattern	Bigrams	MWE	TP	FP	TN	FN	Prec.	Recall	F1
N-A	229	193	176	27	9	17	0.867	0.912	0.889
O-N	164	46	14	23	95	32	0.378	0.304	0.337
PN-PN	117	101	94	15	1	7	0.862	0.931	0.895
A-N	53	21	13	3	29	8	0.813	0.619	0.703
O-O	46	10	5	9	27	5	0.357	0.500	0.417
N-PN	34	16	7	9	9	9	0.438	0.438	0.438
N-N	31	20	11	6	5	9	0.647	0.550	0.595
A-PN	15	13	3	1	1	10	0.750	0.231	0.353
All Pat.	689	420	323	93	176	97	0.776	0.769	0.773

Table 2a: Multi-layer perceptron using Bayesian regulation back-propagation as training function: precision, recall and *F*-measure in the classification of the most common bigram's patterns.

Pattern	Bigrams	MWE	TP	FP	TN	FN	Prec.	Recall	F1
N-A	229	193	191	35	1	2	0.845	0.990	0.912
O-N	164	46	11	6	112	35	0.647	0.239	0.349
PN-PN	117	101	101	16	0	0	0.863	1.000	0.927
A-N	53	21	17	4	28	4	0.810	0.810	0.810
O-O	46	10	0	2	34	10	0.000	0.000	0.000
N-PN	34	16	11	5	13	5	0.688	0.688	0.688
N-N	31	20	16	7	4	4	0.696	0.800	0.744
A-PN	15	13	2	2	0	11	0.500	0.154	0.235
All Pat.	689	420	349	77	192	71	0.819	0.831	0.825

Table 2b: Multi-layer perceptron using Levenberg-Marquardt as training function: precision, recall and *F*-measure in the classification of the most common bigram's patterns.

Pattern	Bigrams	MWE	TP	FP	TN	FN	Prec.	Recall	F1
N-A	229	193	187	33	3	6	0.850	0.969	0.906
O-N	164	46	0	0	118	46	0.720	0.000	0.000
PN-PN	117	101	101	15	1	0	0.871	1.000	0.931
A-N	53	21	17	10	22	4	0.630	0.810	0.708
O-O	46	10	0	0	36	10	0.783	0.000	0.000
N-PN	34	16	2	7	11	14	0.222	0.125	0.160
N-N	31	20	18	8	3	2	0.692	0.900	0.783
A-PN	15	13	2	1	1	11	0.667	0.154	0.250
All Pat.	689	420	327	74	195	93	0.815	0.779	0.797

Table 2c: Multi-layer perceptron using scaled conjugate gradient as training function: precision, recall and *F*-measure in the classification of the most common bigram's patterns.

6 Evaluation of two different tools

Using the same excerpts of our corpus, we proceeded to the evaluation of two different tools for extracting MWEs from text: MWEtoolkit[1] (Ramisch, 2012) and Text-NSP[2] (Banerjee and Pedersen, 2003).

6.1 MWEtoolkit

Before using this tool, we POS-tagged the corpus using TreeTagger[3] (Schmid, 1994), with a Portuguese parameter file. Then we transformed the tagged corpus to the xml format used by MWEtoolkit using MWEtoolkit script treetagger2xml.

After generating the index, we defined the patterns file using the following bigrams patterns: N-N, N-ADJ, N-V, ADJ-ADJ, ADJ-N, ADJ-V, V-V, V-N and V-ADJ. There is not a PN tag for proper name in TreeTagger, so the proper names were treated as nouns (N). And we decided not to use the other grammatical classes (adverbs, pronouns, etc.), labeled as "O" in the previous section, because the only patterns that gave more than 10 MWEs with frequency higher than 3 using those classes were O-N and O-O, and we did not obtain good values for their classification using the multi-layer perceptron classification algorithms.

We used those patterns to generate all the bigrams and we obtained 28,738 candidates, with their frequencies and the frequencies of each word composing the bigram. Then we calculated five different association measures for each candidate: maximum likelihood estimator (mle), pointwise mutual information (pmi), Student's t-test (t), Dice's coefficient (dice), and log-likelihood (ll).

[1] `http://mwetoolkit.sourceforge.net/PHITE.php?sitesig=MWE`

[2] `http://search.cpan.org/~tpederse/Text-NSP/`

[3] `http://www.cis.uni-muenchen.de/~schmid/tools/TreeTagger/`

Then we created candidates files ordered by each of these five association measures and we ranked the n best candidates, n = 50, 100, 500, 1000 and 5000. Finally, we used MWEtoolkit's automatic evaluation script to evaluate each of these ranked candidates against our reference file.

The reference file was created with the 447 MWEs selected according to the method described in Section 4, i. e., all the bigrams that appear three or more times in our corpus and that we manually considered as a MWE. It is important to note that our reference file does not contain all the MWEs with two words in the corpus, since we generated more than 49,000 bigrams and we could not evaluate all of them by hand. Furthermore, the corpus is formed by newspaper texts, treating different subjects, thus it is more difficult to create a closed set of all possible two-word MWEs. Therefore, our evaluation is a comparison of how many of the most frequent two-word MWEs in our corpus are ranked as the n best candidates by each of the association measures.

Table 3 and Figure 1 show the result of our evaluation using the MWEtoolkit. Each number in the table represents how many of the MWEs in our reference list were found among the n best ranked candidates. For example, for the "ll" measure, among the 50 best ranked candidates 27 are MWEs that appear in our reference list.

	dice	**ll**	**mle**	**pmi**	**t**
50	0	27	5	0	11
100	12	55	10	0	31
500	34	152	49	1	105
1000	59	170	87	9	169
5000	161	187	179	94	186

Table 3: MWEtoolkit: number of MWEs among the first n-best candidates, ranked by five association measures.

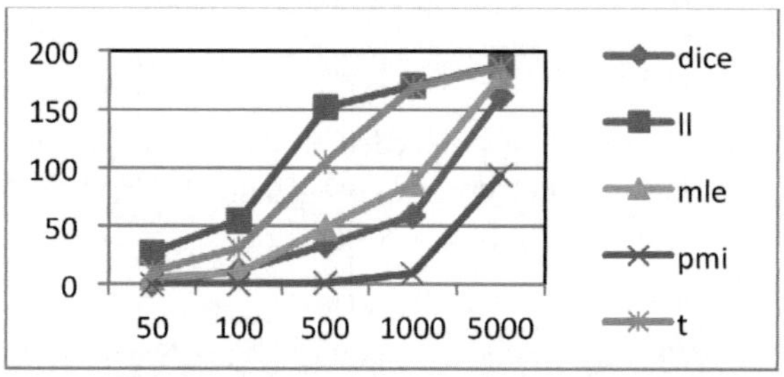

Figure 1: MWEtoolkit: five association measures performance comparison.

ll	**TP**	**Prec.**	**Recall**	**F1**
50	27	0.54	0.06	0.11
100	55	0.55	0.12	0.20
500	152	0.30	0.34	0.32
1000	170	0.17	0.38	0.23
5000	187	0.04	0.41	0.07

Table 4: MWEtoolkit: precision, recall and F-measure for the log-likelihood measure.

Analyzing the results, we notice that with log-likelihood measure we could find the highest number of MWEs present in our reference list, for all values of n. Since our reference list is formed by the most frequent MWEs in the corpus (frequency higher than three), this is an evidence of how suitable this measure is when the task is to find the most frequent two-word MWEs.

Table 4 presents the results of precision, recall and F-measure for the ll-measure for different values of n candidates. However, it should be kept in mind that precision and recall here are based on our reference list, which does not contain all the two-word MWEs in the corpus.

6.2 Text-NSP

Before applying this tool, the only pre-processing performed was to remove the XML tags. The next step was to define a stop words list file, since we are interested in finding MWEs following the patterns N-N, N-ADJ, N-V, like in Sections 4 and 5.

We ran the program using the script "count.pl", giving as parameter the stop words file and the corpus file, and 2 as n-gram value, meaning that we wanted to generate only bigrams.

The exit file is a list of all bigrams in the corpus, and each line contains a bigram, the frequency of the bigram, and the frequency of each of the two words forming the bigram.

Using the exit file and the script "statistics.pl" we generated the candidates' files ranked by four different association measures: Dice's coefficient (dice), log-likelihood (ll), pointwise mutual information (pmi) and Student's t-test (t). Maximum likelihood estimator is not implemented by Text-NSP. Then we transformed each of the candidates files to the XML format used by the MWEtoolkit and we used the MWEtoolkit scripts to create files with the *n* best candidates (n = 50, 100, 500, 1000 and 5000) and to evaluate each of the files against our reference file. Table 5 and Figure 2 show the results of those evaluations.

	dice	ll	pmi	t
50	7	31	0	23
100	7	64	0	39
500	8	241	1	180
1000	11	314	4	331
5000	73	382	15	406

Table 5: Text-NSP: number of MWEs among the first *n*-best candidates, ranked by four association measures.

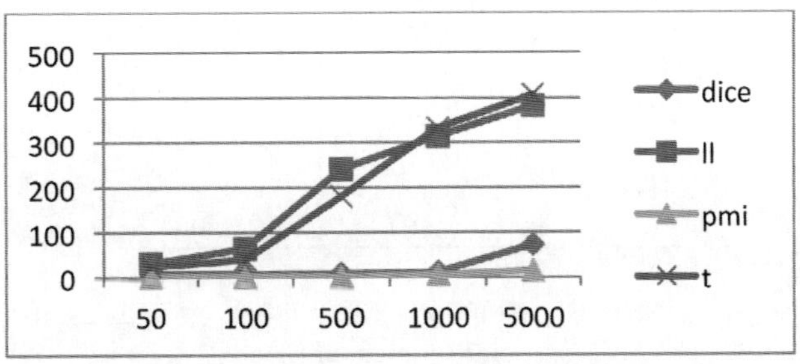

Figure 2: Text-NSP: four association measures performance comparison.

ll	TP	Prec.	Recall	F1
50	31	0.62	0.07	0.12
100	64	0.64	0.14	0.23
500	241	0.48	0.54	0.51
1000	314	0.31	0.70	0.43
5000	382	0.08	0.85	0.14

Table 6: Text-NSP: precision, recall and *F*-measure for the log-likelihood measure.

The results show that for values of n = 50,100, and 500 we obtained the best results using the log-likelihood measure and for n = 1000 and 5000, Student's t-test gave the best results.

Comparing with MWEtoolkit, we had better results with Text-NSP for the log-likelihood and the Student's t-test measures, and weaker results for the dice and pmi measures.

Table 6 shows the precision, recall and *F*-measure that we obtained for the log-likelihood measure. We had very good precision values using the Text-NSP with the log-likelihood measure. For example, from the 50 best ranked candidates by this measure, 31 were MWEs present in our reference list.

6.3 Comparison between MWEtoolkit and Text-NSP

Using the 500 best candidates generated by MWEtoolkit and Text-NSP, ranked by Student's t-test, we analyzed by hand those 500 candidates to decide which ones are Brazilian Portuguese MWEs. Table 7 shows the precision given by each of the tools for the first *n* candidates, *n* = 50, 100, 150...500.

Text-NSP showed higher precision than MWEtoolkit for all values of *n* candidates, especially for the smaller values of *n*. With MWEtoolkit, the precision was around 40%, while with Text-NSP it starts with 62% for the first best 50 candidates and decreases to 48% for the first best 500 candidates.

We can suppose that for an application interested in a small number of Brazilian Portuguese MWE candidates, Text-NSP would be a better choice, and as the number of candidates increases, the programs tend to have similar performance.

Checking the best ranked candidates generated by MWEtoolkit, we noted that it ranked well some bigrams formed by a noun + the preposition "a" (the/fem.), a pattern that is common in a Brazilian Portuguese corpus, but that usually does not form MWEs. This happened, despite not having any pattern that includes preposition in our patterns' list, because the POS-tagger used (TreeTagger) wrongly labelled those "a" prepositions as nouns. The same is true for the pronoun "seu/sua" (his/her), which was labelled as adjective. This can explain the difference in performance between the tools, when comparing the implementation of the same association measures.

As in the tests performed in Section 5, the most common patterns of MWE found by both programs were noun-adjective (e.g. Casa Branca, plano real, Estados Unidos) and proper name-proper name (e.g. Fernando Henrique, Ayrton Senna, Paulo Maluf).

n first cand.	MWEtoolkit	Text-NSP
50	0.34	0.62
100	0.47	0.57
150	0.43	0.55
200	0.41	0.53
250	0.40	0.54
300	0.41	0.53
350	0.37	0.53
400	0.41	0.50
450	0.42	0.52
500	0.40	0.48

Table 7: MWEtoolkit and Text-NSP precision for the first *n* best candidates, using Student's t-test association measure.

7 Conclusions and future work

We obtained very similar results using different algorithms for the classification of MWEs, with bagging, decision trees and multi-layer perceptron having a slightly better performance.

Using multi-layer perceptron with three different training functions, we identified the bigram's patterns that are better classified as MWE. With the function Levenberg-Marquardt we had better results in classifying the pattern noun-adjective (the most common in our corpus) and the function Scaled Conjugate Gradient was the most successful in classifying MWEs following the pattern proper name-proper name.

The comparison between two programs for automatic extraction of MWEs showed that Text-NSP had a better precision than MWEtoolkit, especially for smaller number of candidates. As the number of candidates increases, the difference in performance between the two programs decreases.

It is important to note that MWEtoolkit is more complete, in the sense it implements more statistical measures, makes the comparison between the output candidates file and a reference list file and generates a list of candidates having more complete information, including all the statistical measures of each candidate in the same file, and in a XML format more easily consumable by other programs.

As a future work, we intend to perform a similar comparison of tools and classification algorithms for the extraction of Brazilian Portuguese MWEs, not limiting our candidates to bigrams, but studying n-grams in general, also allowing noncontiguous n-grams.

References

Agarwal, A., Ray, B., Choudhury, M., Sarkar, S., Basu, A.: Automatic Extraction of Multiword Expressions in Bengali: An Approach for Miserly Resource Scenarios. In: *Proceedings of ICON 2004*, pp. 165-174. Macmillan, Basingstoke (2004).

Aha, D. and Kibler, D. (1991). Instance-based learning algorithms. *Machine Learning*. 6:37-66.

Antunes, S. and Mendes, A. MWE in Portuguese - Proposal for a Typology for Annotation in Running Text. *Proceedings of the 9th Workshop on Multiword Expressions (MWE 2013)*, pp. 87–92, Atlanta, Georgia, 13-14 June 2013.

Banerjee, S and Pedersen, T. (2003). The Design, Implementation, and Use of the Ngram Statistic Package. *In Proceedings of th Fourth International Conference on Intelligent Text Processing and Computational Linguistics*, pp. 370-381, Mexico City.

Breiman, L. (2001). Random Forests. *Machine Learning*. 45(1):5-32.

Breiman , L. (1996). Bagging predictors. *Machine Learning*. 24(2):123-140.

CETENFolha (Corpus de Extractos de Textos Electrónicos NILC/Folha de S. Paulo) (2008). Linguateca – Portugal – www.linguateca.pt/ACDC/

Chang, Chih-Chung and Lin, Chih-Jen (2001). LIBSVM - A Library for Support Vector Machines. http://www.csie.ntu.edu.tw/~cjlin/libsvm/.

Choueka, Y. (1988). Looking for needles in a haystack or locating interesting collocational expressions in large textual databases. *In RIAO'88*, pp. 609–624.

Church, K. W. and Hanks, P (1990). Word Association Norms, Mutual Information and Lexicography. *Computational Linguistics*, 16(1):22–29.

Cooper, G. and Herskovits, E. (1992). A Bayesian method for the induction of probabilistic networks from data. *Machine Learning*. 9(4):309-347.

Dias, G. H. and Lopes, J.G.P. (2005). Extracção automática de unidades polilexicais para o português. In: *A Língua Portuguesa no Computador*. São Paulo: Ed. Mercado de Letras.

Freund, Y. and Schapire, R. E (1996). Experiments with a new boosting algorithm. *In: Thirteenth International Conference on Machine Learning, San Francisco*, pp. 148-156.

Hendrickx, I., Mendes, A. and Antunes, S. (2010). Proposal for Multi-Word Expression Annotation in Running Text Portuguese.

Hurskainen, A. (2008). Multiword Expressions and Machine Translation. *Technical Reports in Language Technology Report No 1, 2008 (*http://www.njas.helsinki.fi/salama).

Kinoshita, J., Nascimento Salvador, L.D. and Dantas de Menezes, C., E. (2006). CoGrOO: a Brazilian-Portuguese Grammar Checker based on the CETENFOLHA Corpus. In proceedings of LREC 2006. http://www.pcs.usp.br/~cogroo/papers/Artigo_LREC_2006.pdf

Piao, S., Rayson, P., Archer, D., Wilson, A., and McEnery, T. (2003). Extracting Multiword Expressions with a Semantic Tagger. *In: Workshop on Multiword Expressions: Analysis, Acquisition and Treatment*, at *ACL 2003, 41st Annual Meeting of the Association for Computational Linguistics*, 2003-07-12, Sapporo, Japan.

Quinlan, J. R. (1993). C4.5: Programs for Machine Learning. Morgan Kaufmann Publishers.

Ramisch, C. (2012). A generic and open framework for MWE treatment – from acquisition to applications - Ph.D. Thesis, Universidade Federal do Rio Grande do Sul (UFRGS), Brazil.

Ramisch, C., Schreiner, P., Idiart, M. and Villavicencio, A. (2008). An Evaluation of Methods for the Extraction of Multiword Expressions, *Proceedings of the LREC Workshop Towards a Shared Task for Multiword Expressions (MWE 2008)*, Marrakech, Morocco, June, 2008.

Sag, I., Baldwin, T., Bond, F., Copestake, A. and Flickinger, D. (2002). Multiword expressions: A pain in the neck for NLP. *In Proc. of the 3rd CICLing (CICLing-2002)*, volume 2276/2010 de *LNCS*, pp. 1–15, Mexico City, Mexico.

Schmid, Helmut (1994). Probabilistic Part-of-Speech Tagging Using Decision Trees. *Proceedings of International Conference on New Methods in Language Processing*, Manchester, UK.

Silva, J., and Lopes, G. (1999). A local Maxima Method and a Fair Dispersion Normalization for Extracting Multiword Units. In *6th Meeting on the Mathematics of Language*, pp. 369-381.

Smadja, F. A. (1996). Translating Collocations for Bilingual Lexicons: A Statistical Approach. *Association for Computational Linguistics*, 22 (1):1-38.

Smadja, F. A. (1993). Retrieving collocations from text: Xtract. *Computational Linguistics.*, 19(1):143–177.

Watrin, Patrick and François, Tomas (2011). An N-gram frequency database reference to handle MWE extraction in NLP applications. *Proceedings of the Workshop on Multiword Expressions: from Parsing and Generation to the Real World (MWE 2011)*, pp. 83–91.

Wordsyoudontknow: Evaluation of lexicon-based decompounding with unknown handling

Karolina Owczarzak **Ferdinand de Haan** **George Krupka** **Don Hindle**

Oracle Language Technology
1111 19th Street NW #600, Washington, DC 20036, USA
{karolina.owczarzak,ferdinand.de.haan,george.krupka,
don.hindle}@oracle.com

Abstract

In this paper we present a cross-linguistic evaluation of a lexicon-based decomposition method for decompounding, augmented with a "guesser" for unknown components. Using a gold standard test set, for which the correct decompositions are known, we optimize the method's parameters and show correlations between each parameter and the resulting scores. The results show that even with optimal parameter settings, the performance on compounds with unknown elements is low in terms of matching the expected lemma components, but much higher in terms of correct string segmentation.

1 Introduction

Compounding is a productive process that creates new words by combining existing words together in a single string. It is predominant in Germanic and Scandinavian languages, but is also present in other languages, e.g. Finnish, Korean, or Farsi. Many languages that are not usually thought of as "compounding" nevertheless display marginal presence of compounds, restricted, for instance, to numerical expressions (e.g. Polish *czterogodzinny* 'four-hour'). Depending on a language, compounding can be a very frequent and productive process, in effect making it impossible to list all the compound words in the dictionary. This creates serious challenges for Natural Language Processing in many areas, including search, Machine Translation, information retrieval and related disciplines that rely on matching multiple occurrences of words to the same underlying representation.

In this paper, we present a cross-linguistic evaluation of a lexicon-based decomposition method augmented with a "guesser" for handling unknown components. We use existing lexicons developed at Oracle Language Technology in combination with a string scanner parametrized with language-specific input/output settings. Our focus is on the evaluation that tries to tease apart string segmentation (i.e. finding boundaries between components) and morphological analysis (i.e. matching component parts to known lemmas).

The paper is organized as follows: Section 2 gives an overview of related research; Section 3 describes the compound analyzer used in our experiments; Section 4 presents experimental results; Section 5 contains error analysis and discussion. Section 6 concludes and suggests future research.

2 Related research

Current research on compound splitting is predominantly lexicon-based, with a range of selection methods to choose the most likely decomposition. The lexicons used to identify components are usually collected from large monolingual corpora (Larson et al., 2000; Monz and de Rijke, 2001; Alfonseca et al, 2008; Holz and Biemann, 2008; von Huyssteen and von Zaanen, 2004).

The problem with pure lexicon-based approach without any constraints is that it will produce many spurious decompositions, matching small substrings that happen to be legitimate words in the

Proceedings of the First Workshop on Computational Approaches to Compound Analysis, pages 63–71,
Dublin, Ireland, August 24 2014.

language. Therefore, some approaches introduce maximizing component length (or, conversely, minimizing the number of components) as one of the selection factors (von Huyssteen and von Zaanen, 2004; Holz and Biemann, 2008; Macherey et al., 2011; Larson et al., 2000); others use part of speech to eliminate short components which tend to be function words (Koehn and Knight, 2003; Monz and de Rijke, 2001). In other cases, Named Entity Recognition is used to filter out proper names that should not be decomposed but that can contain frequent short components like "-berg" or "-dorf" (Alfonseca et al., 2008).

Even after removing unlikely small component candidates, there is enough ambiguity in decomposition to warrant further filtering methods. And so, approaches related to Machine Translation use bilingual parallel corpora to find the most likely components by checking whether their translations match elements of the whole compound translation (Koehn and Knight, 2003; Macherey et al., 2011). Other filtering methods are based on combined frequency of the components (Koehn and Knight, 2003; Holz and Biemann, 2008), point-wise mutual information of components, or occurrence of components in related locations, such as anchor text (Alfonseca et al., 2008). A very interesting lexicon-free approach is presented in Aussems et al. (2013), which uses point-wise mutual information to detect likely boundaries between characters that would identify a compound.

A major issue with the current research is the absence of common training and testing data, particularly across multiple languages, which then translates into limited evaluations of presented methods. Using pre-annotated frequency lists, we create gold standard test sets for 10 languages: Norwegian, Danish, Dutch, Estonian, Finnish, German, Hungarian, Korean, Farsi, Swedish, which range from around 600 to 15,000 compounds. This allows a more thorough comparison of the analyser performance across different languages.

3 Lexicon-based analyzer

Our approach follows the main line of research in that it uses lexicons to identify potential components in a compound; however, our lexicons contain lemmas rather than word forms, in contrast to lexicons harvested from monolingual corpora. However, the lexicons we use contain as well as partial lemmas whose occurrences are restricted to compounds (e.g. German verb forms without the final *–en*; for example *schließ-*). In addition, we use morphological rules to map recognized inflected forms to base (lexicon) lemmas. Both the lexicons and the morphological rules have been previously created by computational linguists and native speakers for use in a variety of NLP applications at Oracle Language Technology.

On the most basic level, a compound can be explicitly added to the lexicon, with a specific decomposition and appropriate part of speech and grammatical features; this option is used when the decomposition is irregular or non-obvious, for instance when the component appears in a form that is not directly analyzable to its lemma, as in the example below, which shows irregular plurals and deletion of consonant:

(1) a. Danish: *barn* 'child' plural: *børn*
børnebog barn+e+bog [child-*connector*-book] 'children's book'
b. Norwegian Bokmål: deletion of repeated consonant
musikkorps musikk+korps [music-band] 'music band'

Lexicalized compounds are treated like any other words, and their inflected forms will be recognized. Explicitly adding the compound to the lexicon is also useful when the compound can have multiple decompositions, and we want to restrict the output only to the semantically correct analysis. In Dutch, for instance, the compound part *stem* can refer to the noun *stem* 'voice' or to the root of the verb *stemmen* 'vote'. These readings are distinguished in the lexicon by listing explicit decompositions for compounds that contain the part:

(2) Dutch *stem* N vs. V

a.	stemband	stem#band	[voice-cord]	'vocal cord' (N-N)
b.	stembureau	stemmen#bureau	[vote-station]	'polling station (V-N)

However, adding all compounds to the lexicon is simply unfeasible for many languages where the compounding process is highly productive. For this reason, we also use a compound analyser to identify components in a dynamic manner, based on available component lemmas in the lexicon. Components are found by removing any recognizable inflections from the candidate string, scanning it left-to-right, and looking for all matching lemmas, subject to constraints based on part of speech, length, number of components, and available features. For speed reasons, we apply greedy matching, and prefer decompositions with the longest prefix and the smallest number of components.

Since our goal is developing language processing systems that are as universal as possible, leaving context-dependent decisions to higher-level applications, we are not particularly concerned with always selecting the single best decomposition for a compound, since in many cases is will be dependent on the domain and application. However, it is useful to filter out decompositions that would be highly unlikely in any context, for instance those containing small function words mentioned in previous section. For this purpose, we apply constraints described below.

3.1 Rules for compound sequences

For each language, we list the possible part of speech sequences that can appear in compounds. These rules serve not only to prevent the decompositions that would not appear in the language (for instance, *noun-verb-particle*), but also to restrict sequences that are fairly infrequent, but that would lead to considerable over-generation if they were added. For example, in German, there are relatively few compounds that end with a verb, unless it is a combination of movable prefix particle (*aus*, *an*, *ab*, *ein*, etc.) and the verb (*aus+gehen*, *auf+stehen*, *um+steigen*, etc.). These verbs are functionally analyzed as compounds, i.e. a concatenation of two lemmas. However, since sequences noun/adjective/verb + verb are much less productive (*spazieren+gehen*, *auto+fahren*), it is more efficient to restrict the verb-final compounds to *particle-verb* only, and add the exceptions to the lexicon. A few examples of compound part of speech sequences for different languages are shown in (3).

(3) a. Dutch:
cardinal_number + verb e.g., *vier+en+delen* 'quarter'
b. Estonian:
noun+adjective e.g. *silmi+pimestav* 'eye-dazzling'
c. German:
ordinal_number + adjective e.g. *zweit+größt* 'second largest'
d. Swedish:
noun + noun e.g *citron+saft* 'lemon juice'

Another issue is compounds of cardinal or ordinal numbers, which can also occur in some languages like Italian (*cinquecento+sessanta+nove* 'five hundred sixty nine') or Greek (*οκτακόσιοι*, *οκτώ* + *ακόσιοι* 'eight hundred'). These number compounds can be very productive and are also included in the lists of allowed compound sequences.

3.2 Connectors

In many compounding languages, the subparts of a compound can be connected with extra material, a connector (or linking element). These are semantically empty elements that have a mainly phonological role in connecting the compound parts (Bauer, 2009). In many Germanic languages connectors are derived from plural or genitive morphemes (such as *–er* or *–s* in German), but do not have this role any more, as evidenced, among others, by the fact that in certain cases the connector is optional and compounds with and without a connector co-exist (4a) or by the fact that there are cases where two different connectors co-occur (4b) (Krott et al., 2007):

(4) a. Norwegian Bokmål:
rettssak rett + s + sak 'court case'
rettsak rett + Ø + sak
b. Dutch:
paddestoel pad + e + stoel 'toadstool'
paddenstoel pad + en + stoel

For each language, we create a set of allowed connectors, a few examples of which can be seen in (5).[1] Note that it might be useful to restrict certain connectors to appear only in certain sequences (e.g. between noun and noun, but not adjective and verb); we plan to implement this restriction in future work.

(5) Connector examples

a.	Dutch	**s**	e.g. *water+s+nood* 'flood'
b.	German	**zu**	e.g. to match *auf+stehen* and *auf+zu+stehen* 'stand up'
c.	Swedish	**o**	e.g. *veck+o+slut* 'weekend'

3.3 Decompounding settings

Another factor in successful dynamic decompounding is restrictions on possible number of components, and on length of candidate strings and candidate components. Choosing to allow fewer components of longer length helps to prevent spurious over-analysis, where several short words can accidentally match the string which is being analyzed. However, setting the limits too high might also prevent legitimate decomposition, so this trade-off needs to be carefully balanced. There are four basic length settings, as shown in Table 1 below; the values are dependent on language.

Maximum number of elements: Limits the number of components in a compound. Low values help prevent spurious decompositions into many small elements.

Minimum length of compound: The minimum length of string that should be subject to decompounding; short strings are unlikely to be compounds, so for efficiency reasons, they are not decompounded.

Minimum length of component: Specifies the minimum length of potential compound elements; shorter substrings are excluded to avoid accidental matching of very short words.

Minimum length of component with connector: A version of the above setting, it specifies the minimum length of potential element when this element is next to a connector; to avoid spurious matches of the short word + connector combination (e.g. Dutch *paspoort* should be decomposed as *pas+poort*, not *pa+s+poort*).

setting	**value**
maximum number of elements	2-4
minimum length of compound	4-11
minimum length of component	2-4
minimum length of component with connector	2-4

Table 1. Length settings for dynamic decompounding.

The values for these settings are established manually and separately for each language, based on review of top N most frequent compounds in the lexicon and the general knowledge of that language's grammar and patterns.

4 Experimental results

Despite all the constraints and settings described above, decompounding is still an imperfect process: there can be multiple competing (i.e. overlapping) decompositions, and many decompositions that are technically possible are incorrect due to semantic reasons. This problem becomes even more challenging when some of the components are not present in the lexicon. Since lexicons are limited, and real world text can contain misspellings, proper names, or obscure words, we need to address the issue of decompounding with unknown elements. Therefore, we set out to evaluate the performance of our lexicon-based method on a gold standard set of known compounds, and compare it to an augmented version that also tries to construct potential components from unknown substrings.

[1] Note that for our purposes, particle *zu* in German is also treated as a connector, to match the movable particle verbs that can appear with and without *zu*: *auf* + *zu* + *stehen* and *auf* + *stehen* 'get up'.

4.1 Test set

For our experiments, we collected compounds from the top 90% frequency lists based on large news and Wikipedia corpora. Each compound was annotated with the correct decomposition(s) by a linguist who was also a native speaker of the target language according to simple instructions: if the meaning of the word is compositional (i.e. can be fully described by the component elements), treat it as a compound and provide component lemmas.

Approximate sizes of source corpora per language are given in Table 2; column "compounds" shows the count of compounds; column "lexical" shows how many of these are lexicalized compounds (i.e. compounds that have been added to the lexicon for reasons of irregularity). While two-part compounds are by far the most frequent in all the languages we examined, there is also some percentage of compounds with more than two parts; the distribution is shown in the last four columns.

language	news corpus MB	wiki corpus MB	compounds	lexical	2-part	3-part	4-part	5-part
Danish	335	154	1,982	1,326	1,856	122	4	0
Dutch	512	103	3,439	1,909	3,186	245	8	0
Estonian	204	41	2,343	562	2,166	169	8	0
Farsi	512	244	648	340	635	13	0	0
Finnish	512	78	1,868	1,665	1,703	154	11	0
German	520	227	15,490	5,087	14,544	915	31	0
Hungarian	512	257	1,841	1,537	1,794	45	2	0
Korean	826	190	11,398	4,774	10,919	425	39	5
Norwegian	512	88	3,582	1,106	3,405	175	2	0
Swedish	512	204	9,677	5,608	8,901	744	31	5

Table 2. Size of corpora per language, count of compounds, distribution of parts.

4.2 Dynamic decompounding with available lemmas

As mentioned before, it is not feasible to add all (or even the majority) of possible compounds, so we need to examine our performance using only dynamic decompounding. For this purpose, we removed all lexicalized compounds from the lexicon, and then ran the analyzer on the compound test set described above. This means that all the compound analysis was done dynamically, using only the available simple lemmas and compound rules and length restrictions. Table 3 shows the results. The scores for lexicalized + dynamic decompounding are given only for reference; they are high but less interesting, since they reflect the fact that the lexicalized compounds were largely collected from the same corpora (among other sources). Our focus is on the dynamic scores, which show performance on unknown compounds assuming a nearly "perfect" lexicon that contains almost all the component lemmas. As such, these scores will serve as the upper bound for our next experiment, in which we remove at least one of the component lemmas from the lexicon and test the resulting performance.

As can be seen in Table 3, for most languages recall decreases considerably – this suggests that lexicalized compounds are of the kind that are not covered by the decompounding rules or whose correct analysis is blocked by another decomposition.

4.3 Dynamic decompounding with missing lemmas

While dynamic decompounding can handle the productive nature of compounds, it is still limited to finding components that are already present in the lexicon. However, in the real world compounds will contain elements unknown to a lexicon-based analyzer, whether it is because they are domain-specific vocabulary, proper names, foreign borrowings, or misspellings. In those cases, it is still useful to attempt analysis and return the known parts, with the option of returning the unknown substring as the missing lemma.

	lexicalized + dynamic			dynamic only		
	prec	rec	f-score	prec	rec	f-score
Danish	98.18	99.6	98.88	87.99	66.9	76.01
Dutch	98.84	100	99.42	84.46	80.49	82.43
Estonian	98.25	99.83	99.03	95.69	90.27	92.9
Farsi	92.9	100	96.32	65.75	72.84	69.11
Finnish	98.74	100	99.37	84.55	68.63	75.76
German	96.11	99.98	98.01	88.01	89.03	88.52
Hungarian	90.44	99.84	94.91	77.42	72.19	74.71
Korean	99.72	100	99.86	95.23	59.49	73.23
Norwegian	99.6	100	99.8	93.25	86.32	89.65
Swedish	96.35	99.88	98.08	86.67	75.75	80.84

Table 3. Precision, recall, and f-measure for dynamic decompounding.

To evaluate the performance of our analyzer in case where some component lemmas are unknown, we applied a "compound guesser" function that tries to find known elements of unknown compounds, even if a complete decomposition to only known elements is impossible. The guesser has its own constraints, independent of the main compound analyzer, which are shown in Table 4.

setting	value
maximum number of elements	2-20
minimum length of compound	3-20
minimum length of component	2-5
minimum length of unknown element	1-5
minimum percent of string covered	0-100%

Table 4. Settings for dynamic decompounding with unknown elements.

The first three settings are parallel to the settings for regular dynamic decompounding; however, we also add restrictions on length for unknown elements (*minimum length of unknown element*) and total string coverage (*minimum percent of string covered*). Restriction on length of unknown element mean that any unknown string shorter than the minimum length will be treated as a potential connector/suffix/prefix and will not be returned as a lemma:

(6) German: assuming *freundlicher* 'friendlier' is unknown:
umweltfreundlicher -> umwelt + freundlich (! + er)   [environment + friendly]

The last setting allows a more fine-grained control over the proportion of known to unknown parts; however, since any value less than 100% will restrict the number of produced candidate decompositions, resulting in no output if the unknown substring is too long, we do not test the impact of this setting.

For this experiment, we collected all component lemmas from the test compounds, and removed from lexicon at least one component lemma per compound. This renders the whole string unanalyzable by regular means. Then we ran the compound guesser with each combination of settings from Table 4, to find the optimal set of values.

Table 5 shows results obtained with the optimal guesser settings per language, compared to scores from Table 3: a fully functional decomposition that has access to both dynamic decomposition and lexicalized compounds, and dynamic decomposition with near-perfect component lexicon. It is clear that even with optimal settings, the guesser performance falls well below the level of full functionality, even when we compare to a system that has no access to lexicalized compounds. The highest score achieved by the guesser is 34 for the Hungarian test set, which includes mostly simple two-part compounds, and where the lexicon does not provide too many spurious sub-matches.

language	**lexical + dynamic**	**dynamic only**	**dynamic guesser**	**dynamic guesser - string segmentation**
Danish	98.88	76.01	25.93	**51.25**
Dutch	99.42	82.43	27.13	**64.01**
Estonian	99.03	92.9	9.56	**53.89**
Farsi	96.32	69.11	27.16	**78.68**
Finnish	99.37	75.76	19.49	**51.6**
German	98.01	88.52	25.1	**52.29**
Hungarian	94.91	74.71	34	**53.5**
Korean	99.86	73.23	16.81	**76.54**
Norwegian	99.8	89.65	22.56	**49.74**
Swedish	98.08	80.84	25.56	**54.18**

Table 5. Dynamic decomposition with missing lemmas, optimal settings; string segmentation shows accuracy score; remaining values are harmonic f-score of precision and recall.

However, a major problem with this evaluation is that output of the regular decompounding process produces lemmas in their dictionary form, without inflection, whereas the guesser can only return surface strings for the unknown elements which might carry grammatical inflection or stem alternations. Therefore, it would be more fair to compare the guesser to dynamic decompounding in terms of pure string segmentation – whether it finds the same boundaries between components, without concern for the form of the returned component. This lets us tease apart the impact of finding component elements from the impact of morphology. The last column in Table 5 shows accuracy of guesser string segmentation as compared to string segmentation performed by regular dynamic decompounding; in this respect the guesser's performance is indeed much better. These results are encouraging, showing that we can recover correct components in up to 79% of cases, which is a very useful improvement for the purposes of information retrieval and search. While some recall is lost by returning strings instead of lemmas, we are planning to add a second step that would employ a lemma "guesser", in order to produce the most likely dictionary form from the recovered unknown string.

language	**max elements**	**corr. with score**	**min length of compound**	**corr. with score**	**min length of element**	**corr. with score**	**min length of unknown element**	**corr. with score**
Danish	2	-0.19	3-7	-0.46	4	0.43	3	-0.09
Dutch	2	-0.21	8	-0.47	5	0.51	3	-0.06
Estonian	2	-0.15	3-7	-0.57	4	0.33	3	-0.08
Farsi	2	-0.17	3-5	-0.51	3	0.11	2	-0.24
Finnish	2-10	-0.07	3-8	-0.49	5	0.41	3	0
German	2	-0.26	8	-0.43	5	0.5	3	-0.06
Hungarian	2-16	0	1-6	-0.58	4	0.39	2	-0.33
Korean	2-10	-0.07	3	-0.14	2	-0.07	1	-0.11
Norwegian	2-10	-0.18	3-8	-0.61	5	0.56	3	0.01
Swedish	2	-0.23	7	-0.45	4	0.49	3	-0.04
Average		**-0.15**		**-0.47**		**0.37**		**-0.1**

Table 6. Optimal guesser settings and their correlations of settings with the guesser score.

Finally, Table 6 shows the correlation (Pearson's r) of guesser settings (or their ranges) and the resulting scores. As can be seen, the strongest correlation holds for the minimum length of compound (average -0.47) and minimum length of element (0.37). In the former case, the correlation is inverse, which means the higher the value, the lower the final score; this is caused by the fact that our test set contains only compounds, so returning the whole unsplit string will never be the right result. The second correlation reflects the fact that it is safer to exclude very short elements from appearing as components, a finding that confirms earlier research.

5 Error analysis

A considerable percentage of mismatch errors when guessing the unknown components of compounds is caused by the connectors. Our current guesser settings return the whole unknown string, without attempting to identify any potential connectors on its edges. This seems like an obvious area for improvement, as it would let us return more correct decompositions for cases shown in Table 7 (unknown strings are enclosed in square brackets and are currently returned whole).

language	token	dynamic	guesser	translation
Norwegian	kjærlighetsbrev	kjærlighet#brev	kjærlighet#[**s** + brev]	love letter
Danish	ungdomshus	ungdom#hus	ungdom#[**s** + hus]	youth
German	sklavenmoral	sklave#moral	sklave#[**n** + moral]	slave morality
Swedish	kvinnoförbund	kvinna#förbund	kvinn#[**o** + förbund]	women's alliance

Table 7. Examples of connector mismatches between dynamic decompounding and the guesser.

As could be expected, most errors are nevertheless caused by the guesser splitting unknown strings into smaller known chunks; several typical examples are shown in Table 8.

language	token	dynamic	guesser	translation
Danish	populærkulturen	populær#kultur	populær#kult#uren	popular culture
Dutch	kunstschilders	kunst#schilder	kunst#schil#ders	painters
Finnish	rockmuusikot	rock#muusiko	rock#muusi#kot	rock music
Swedish	radioversion	radio#version	radio#vers#ion	radio version

Table 8. Examples of incorrect splitting of unknown strings.

6 Conclusion and future work

In this paper, we have shown a dictionary-based compound analyzer, augmented with the function to handle unknown substrings. A cross-linguistic evaluation against the gold standard containing component lemmas shows that the correct handling of unknown compound elements is a difficult issue especially if we try to match dictionary lemmas; however, a more detailed evaluation of the string segmentation and boundary detection shows fairly good results. Being able to decompose unknown compounds and match the components to known lemmas to increase recall is crucial to many NLP applications, such as information retrieval or Machine Translation. A correct segmentation is of fundamental importance, but the question remains how we can match the unknown, possibly inflected, substring to known lemmas. In the future, we plan to address this question by (1) adding the option to separate out connectors from unknown strings, and (2) build a lemma "guesser" that would try to construct a probable dictionary representation for the unknown string, in effect building a pipeline that would more fully mirror the process of regular dynamic decompounding.

Acknowledgements

We would like to thank the rest of the Oracle Language Technology team, in particular Elena Spivak and Rattima Nitisaroj, for their help with compound examples.

References

Alfonseca, Enrique, Slaven Bilac and Stefan Pharies. 2008. German Decompounding in a Difficult Corpus. In *Computational Linguistics and Intelligent Text Processing*, A. Gelbukh (ed.). Springer Verlag, Berlin and Heidelberg, 128-139.

Aussems, Suzanne., Bas Goris., Vincent Lichtenberg, Nanne van Noord, Rick Smetser, and Menno van Zaanen. 2013. Unsupervised identification of compounds. In *Proceedings of the 22nd Belgian-Dutch conference on machine learning*, A. van den Bosch, T. Heskes, & D. van Leeuwen (Eds.), Nijmegen, 18-25.

Bauer, Laurie. 2009. Typology of Compounds. In *The Oxford Handbook of Compounding*, Rochelle Lieber and Pavol Štekauer (eds.). Oxford University Press, Oxford.343-356.

Holz, Florian and Chris Biemann. 2008. Unsupervised and Knowledge-Free Learning of Compound Splits and Periphrases. *CICLing'08 Proceedings of the 9th international conference on Computational linguistics and intelligent text processing*, A. Gelbukh (ed.). Springer Verlag, Berlin and Heidelberg, 117-127.

Koehn, Philipp and Kevin Knight. 2003. Empirical Methods for Compound Splitting. *Proceedings of the 10th conference of the European Chapter of the Association for Computational Linguistics*, Vol. 1, 187-193.

Krott, Andrea, Robert Schreuder, R. Harald Baayen and Wolfgang U. Dressler. 2007 Analogical effects on linking elements in German compounds. *Language and Cognitive Processes*, 22(1):25-57.

Larson, Martha, Daniel Willett, Joachin Köhler and Gerhard Rigoll. 2000. Compound splitting and lexical unit recombination for improved performance of a speech recognition system for German parliamentary speeches In *INTERSPEECH*, 945-948.

Macherey, Klaus, Andrew M. Dai, David Talbot, Ashok C. Popat and Franz Och. 2011. Language-independent compound splitting with Morphological Operations. *Proceedings of the 49th Annual Meeting of the Association for Computational Linguistics*, 1395-1404.

Monz, Christof and Maarten de Rijke. 2002. Shallow Morphological Analysis in Monolingual Information Retrieval for Dutch, German and Italian. In Evaluation *of Cross-Language Information Retrieval Systems*. Carol Peters, Martin Braschler, Julio Gonzalo and Michael Kluck (eds.). Springer Verlag, Berlin and Heidelberg, 262-277.

van Huyssteen, Gerhard and Menno van Zaanen. 2004. Learning Compound Boundaries for Afrikaans Spelling Checking. In *Pre-Proceedings of the Workshop on International Proofing Tools and Language Technologies*; Patras, Greece. 101–108.

van Zaanen, Menno, Gerhard van Huyssteen, Suzanne Aussems, Chris Emmery, and Roald Eiselen. 2014. The Development of Dutch and Afrikaans Language Resources for Compound Boundary Analysis. In *Proceeding of LREC 2014.*

Multiword noun compound bracketing using Wikipedia

Caroline Barrière   **Pierre André Ménard**
Centre de Recherche Informatique de Montréal (CRIM)
Montréal, QC, Canada
{caroline.barriere;pierre-andre.menard}@crim.ca

Abstract

This research suggests two contributions in relation to the multiword noun compound bracketing problem: first, demonstrate the usefulness of Wikipedia for the task, and second, present a novel bracketing method relying on a word association model. The intent of the association model is to represent combined evidence about the possibly lexical, relational or coordinate nature of links between all pairs of words within a compound. As for Wikipedia, it is promoted for its encyclopedic nature, meaning it describes terms and named entities, as well as for its size, large enough for corpus-based statistical analysis. Both types of information will be used in measuring evidence about lexical units, noun relations and noun coordinates in order to feed the association model in the bracketing algorithm. Using a gold standard of around 4800 multiword noun compounds, we show performances of 73% in a strict match evaluation, comparing favourably to results reported in the literature using unsupervised approaches.

1 Introduction

The noun compound bracketing task consists in determining related subgroups of nouns within a larger compound. For example (from Lauer (1995)), *(woman (aid worker))* requires a right-bracketing interpretation, contrarily to *((copper alloy) rod)* requiring a left-bracketing interpretation. When only three words are used, *n1 n2 n3*, bracketing is defined as a binary decision between grouping *(n1,n2)* or grouping *(n2,n3)*. Two models, described in early work by Lauer (1995), are commonly used to inform such decision: the adjacency model and the dependency model. The former compares probabilities (or more loosely, strength of association) of two alternative adjacent noun compounds, that of *n1 n2* and of *n2 n3*. The latter compares probabilities of two alternative dependencies, either between *n1* and *n3* or between *n2* and *n3*.

Most compound bracketing research has focused on three-noun compounds as described above. Some recent work (Pitler et al. (2010), Vadas and Curran (2007b)) looks at larger compounds, experimenting with a dataset created by Vadas and Curran (2007a) which we also use in our research. For larger noun compounds, the adjacency model alone will not allow longer range dependencies to be taken into account. This had been noted much earlier in Barker (1998) using examples such as *(wooden (((French (onion soup)) bowl) handle))* to show a long-range dependency between *wooden* and *handle*.

To allow for such long-range dependencies, our bracketing algorithm looks at all possible word associations within the full expression to make its decisions. The word associations are captured within an association model which goes beyond the adjacency and dependency models. The association model represents combined evidence about the possibly lexical, relational or coordinate nature of the links between all word pairs. In its current implementation, our association model relies on Wikipedia as a resource for obtaining all three types of evidence. Wikipedia is used in two forms: first as a list of terms and named entities (Wikipedia page titles), and second, as a large corpus obtained from the merging of all its pages. The resulting corpus is large enough to be used for statistical measures. The most current version contains 14,466,099 pages in English for an uncompressed file size of 47 gigabytes (including

Proceedings of the First Workshop on Computational Approaches to Compound Analysis, pages 72–80,
Dublin, Ireland, August 24 2014.

some metadata). To the best of our knowledge, no previous research has used Wikipedia for the noun bracketing task, and this research will explore its usefulness.

The reminder of this article will unfold as follows. Section 2 presents a brief literature review. Section 3 describes the dataset used in our experiments. Section 4 presents the bracketing algorithm, and Section 5 the implementation of a word association model using Wikipedia. Section 6 describes our evaluation approach, while results are presented and analysed in Section 7. Section 8 concludes and suggests future work.

2 Related work

Noun compound bracketing has not received as much attention as many other Natural Language Processing (NLP) tasks. Nakov and Hearst (2005) call it an understudied language analysis problem. Early work by Lauer (1995) took inspiration in even earlier linguistic work by Levi (1978). Lauer (1995) having devised a small dataset of 3-word noun compounds, his dataset was reused by various researchers (Lapata et al. (2004), Girju et al. (2005), Nakov and Hearst (2005)) who promoted the use of corpus-based empirical methods for the task.

To address the noun compound bracketing task, different authors use different datasets, different views on the problem (adjacency, dependency), different methods of resolution (supervised, unsupervised) and different constraints on the problem (compound seen in isolation or in context). Independently of such differences, all researchers have an interest in evaluating word-pair associations. Most recent research uses the Web for providing word pair association scores to their bracketing algorithm. The work of Lapata et al. (2004) shows usefulness of web counts for different tasks, including noun compound bracketing. The work of Pitler et al. (2010) intensively uses web-scale ngrams in a supervised task for large NP bracketing, showing that coverage impacts on accuracy. Beyond bigram counts on the web, varied and clever searches (Nakov and Hearst, 2005) have been suggested such as the use of paraphrases (*n1 causes n2*) or simpler possessive markers (*n1's n2*) or even the presence of an hyphen between words (*n1-n2*). All variations are to provide better word association estimates and improve bracketing. The use of web counts is sometimes complemented by the use of more structured resources, such as in Vadas and Curran (2007b) who combines web counts with features from Wordnet.

In our research, instead of web counts, we rely on a community-based encyclopedic resource, Wikipedia, for corpus-based evidence. We rely on the same resource to access a list of terms and entities. Although not much of the structure of Wikipedia is used in our current implementation, such as its categories or page links, we can envisage to use it in future work. Similarly to other researchers mentioned above, our goal is to gather evidence for word-pair association, although an important contribution of our work is to refine this notion of word-pair association into three subtypes of association: lexical, relational and coordinate. We suggest that a better characterization of the possible links among word pairs in a large compound will better inform the bracketing algorithm.

3 Dataset

Vadas and Curran (2007a) manually went through the Penn Treebank (Marcus et al., 1994) to further annotate large NPs. They openly published a *diff file* of the Penn Treebank to show their annotations which differ from the original. From this available file, we constructed our gold-standard dataset by extracting large NPs (three or more words) which only include relevant items (common and proper nouns, adverbs and adjectives), removing determiners, numbers, punctuations and conjunctions. The expressions were then verified for completeness, so that the opening bracket should be closed within the length of text defined in the differential file. Finally, tags and single words enclosing parentheses were removed to produce simplified versions of the bracketed expressions (e.g *(NML (NNP Nesbitt) (NNP Thomson) (NNP Deacon))* becomes *(Nesbitt (Thomson Deacon)))*.

Vadas and Curran (2007a) used a Named Entity annotator to suggest bracketing to the human annotators (who could accept or reject them). The entity types used were the ones defined by Weischedel and Ada Brunstein (2005) (e.g. Person, Facility, Organization, Nationality, Product, Event, etc). Named entities could be kept *as-is* by the annotators or could be bracketed if deemed compositional. Annotators were also instructed to use a default right-bracketing (implicit in Penn Treebank) for difficult decision.

In our dataset, we transformed the ones left *as-is* into right-bracketed in order to have all expressions fully bracketed. This process might seem controversial, as it assumes compositionality of all named entities, which for sure, is a wrong hypothesis. The alternative, though, would require the bracketing algorithm to recognize named entities, which we consider outside the scope of this research. Furthermore, it would also be wrong to assume all named entities are non-compositional. For example *New York Stock Exchange* is clearly compositional, and a Named Entity Tagger based on Wikipedia would easily identify it as a named entity (although the use of Wikipedia as a source of named entities is also debatable). Clearly, no solution is satisfying. We opted for the approximation which provided a fully bracketed gold standard to which our results could be compared. We are aware that this will have a negative impact, in some cases, on our results.

The extraction produced a total 6,600 examples from which we removed duplicate expressions, yielding a corpus of 4,749 unique expressions. Among those unique expressions, 2,889 (60.95%) were three words long (e.g. *Mary Washington College*), 1,270 (26.79%) had four words (e.g. *standardized achievement tests scores*), 413 (8.71%) with five words (e.g. *annual gross domestic product growth*) and the remaining longer expressions (up to nine words) covered around 3.5% of the dataset[1].

4 Bracketing method

As in the work of Pitler et al. (2010), our bracketing algorithm takes into account all possible word pairs within the noun compound. This differs from Barker's algorithm Barker (1998) used in Vadas and Curran (2007b) which only uses local information, three-words at a time, in a right-to-left moving window. We briefly present our algorithm below and refer the reader to Ménard and Barrière (2014) for a more detailed explanation.

First, a list (L1) is created to contain every word pair that can be generated, in order, from an expression. For example, a list L1 {(A,B), (A,C), (A,D), (B,C), (B,D), (C,D)} would be created from expression "A B C D". Second, a dependency score needs to be assigned to each pair. Our bracketing algorithm actually builds a dependency tree and requires these dependency scores. We make the assumption that dependencies are implicitly directed left-to-right. This is an oversimplification, as there are a few cases, such as *Vitamin C* or *Cafe Vienna*, pointed in (Nakov, 2013), where the direction is reversed. Furthermore, this hypothesis is valid only for English and renders our algorithm less applicable to other languages. Although fair for English, this hypothesis should be revisited in future work.

The next step is building a final list of dependencies (L2) to represent the full dependency tree. To do so, the algorithm repeatedly selects from L1 the word pair with the maximum score and adds it to L2 only if both (a) the modifier has not already been used, and (b) the new pair does not create a crossing of modifier/head pairs in the expression. For example, if L2 already contains (AB)(C(DE)), then (BD) would create an invalid crossing and is not accepted. The selection of pairs from L1 ends when all words from the expression, except for the right-most one, are used as modifiers in L2.

Our algorithm is greedy and considers only the best score at every step. We have experimented with randomized greedy algorithms as well, choosing randomly between top N scores at each step, but since results did not improve, we do not report on them in the current article. The bracketing algorithm favours high dependency scores without consideration for the actual distance between word pairs in the source expression. This helps linking far reaching dependencies in noun compounds, but might also force some strong association between two distant words without regard to the soundness of using nearer words.

5 Implementing an association model using Wikipedia

Our association model contains three types of association: lexical, relational and coordinate. Each one will be measured using Wikipedia through different approximation strategies. The challenge is the integration of the association model with the bracketing algorithm. We mainly explore a solution of **score**

[1]We describe our dataset in more details in Ménard and Barrière (2014), and our extraction method is published as part of the LREC resources sharing effort.

modulation which does not require the bracketing algorithm to be modified but rather use the three association scores to modulate the dependency score required by the bracketing algorithm. We present below a basic dependency score, and then different strategies to transform the three types of association into modulation factors on that dependency score.

Basic dependency association: Based simply on the co-occurrence of two words in a corpus, this basic association will be influenced by the actual corpus (domain and size), and the association measure used. In our current experiment, Wikipedia pages are merged into a large corpus (47 Gigabytes) covering multiple domains. As for the association measure, we compare Dice and Point-Wise Mutual Information (PMI), although many more exist in the literature. Co-occurrence is not a direct measure of dependency, it is an approximation. A true dependency measure would require a syntactic analysis (using a link parser) of the whole corpus. We will explore this idea in future work.

Relational association: The relational association is a refinement to the dependency association. In semantic analysis of noun compounds, an important goal is to characterize the nature of the dependence between its words, such as cause, purpose, location, etc (see work by Girju et al. (2005), Nakov and Hearst (2005), Nastase et al. (2013) among many). Here, we do not require the identity relations, but rather search for indications of the relational status of a word pair. In our current implementation, relational association is naïvely determined by the presence of a preposition between two nouns. We use the prepositions: about, at, by, for, from, in, of, on, to, with. We search in the corpus for patterns such as "N1 *at* N2" and "N1 *for* N2", etc. The frequency of these will be used to boost the basic dependency association scores.

Coordinate association: Proximity sometimes refers implicitly to coordination, as for example the words *cotton* and *polyester* in the expression *cotton polyester shirt*. Explicit external evidence that these words often co-occur in a coordination relation could lower their dependency association in expressions such as *cotton polyester shirt*. To gather such evidence, we measure the frequency of explicit coordination between word pairs in Wikipedia. The common conjunctions: *or*, *and*, *nor* are used. We search in the corpus for patterns such as "N1 *or* N2" and "N1 *and* N2", etc. Contrarily to relational associations boosting the basic dependency association scores, coordinate associations should attenuate the dependency scores.

Lexical association: Based on the idea that many compounds, even named entities, are compositional, we want to determine the likeliness that a subexpression in a compound forms itself a lexical unit with a meaning of its own. To do so, we use a first approach requiring a set of corpus-based statistical approximations and a second approach requiring Wikipedia page titles.

- *Statistical approximation*: The presence of determiners (*a, an, the*) and plural forms are used as statistical evidence of lexical association. For example, starting with expression *cotton polyester shirt*, corpus analysis shows that *the cotton shirts* is frequent, which can be used to boost the dependency score between *cotton* and *shirt*. On the other hand, *the cotton polyesters* will be much less frequent. The presence of indicators (determiners and plurals) can be used independently, searching for patterns such as "*the* N1 N2" and "N1 plural(N2)", or together for patterns such as "*a* N1 plural(N2)".

- *Presence in Wikipedia*: A second strong indicator of lexical association for a word pair is its presence in an encyclopedic resource (Wikipedia). In fact, not only word pairs, but for any subcompound of two or more words are considered for look-up as Wikipedia entries. Since we now have lexical units of any length, rather than word pairs, our score modulation is not as straight forward. We thought of two different strategies.

  The first strategy, in line with score modulation, uses all word pairs found in the lexical units to boost dependency scores. For example, assuming the compound *ABCDE*, with *[BCD]* found as a lexical unit in Wikipedia. Then, the association scores of pairs *[BC],[CD],[BD]* are boosted equally (uniform boost). This will not help for any internal bracketing of *[BCD]*, but will reinforce the fact that *[BCD]* should stay together within the larger compound. A variant to uniform boost

Gold	Evaluated	Gold elements		Strict	Lenient	
		Subexpression	Binary tree		Subexpression	Binary tree
(a b) c	(a b) c	(a b)	a-b, b-c	100%	100%	100%
(a b) c	a (b c)	(a b)	a-b, b-c	0%	0%	50%
(a b) (c d)	(a b) (c d)	(a b), (c d)	a-b, c-d, b-d	100%	100%	100%
(a b) (c d)	a (b (c d))	(a b), (c d)	a-b, b-d, c-d	0%	50%	66.6%
(((a b) c) d) (e f)	a (b (c (d (e f))))	(a b), (a b c), (a b c d), (e f)	a-b, b-c, c-d, d-f, e-f	0%	25%	40%
			Average:	40%	55%	71.3%

Table 1: Applied examples of evaluation metrics.

is a right-attachment boost to mimic the default right bracketing in the gold standard for the longer units.

The second strategy is one of **compound segmentation**, in which lexical units found become segmentation constraints on the bracketing algorithm. Association scores are them measured between pairs of lexical units instead of between words pairs. We also try to minimize the number of entities within the compound. For example, assuming again we wish to bracket compound *ABCDE*, and find the possible three segmentations into lexical units using Wikipedia: (1)*[AB][CDE]*, (2) *[AB][CD][E]*, (3) *[ABC][DE]*. Only segmentations (1) and (3) are kept since they have two lexical units and not three. The association scores must then be calculated between pairs of lexical units, and within each lexical unit containing three words or more (to perform full bracketing). Bracketing within a lexical unit will be performed using the same bracketing methods described above. Bracketing between lexical units requires association scores between these units. For doing so, using the example above, we will search in corpus for cooccurrences of *[AB]* with *[CDE]* for segmentation (1), and *[ABC]* with *[DE]* for segmentation (3). Since statistics on longer units will be sparse in the corpus, we will also measure association scores between heads of the lexical units. For example, in segmentation (1) the association between heads *[B]* and *[E]* would be measured.

6 Evaluation metrics

Three methods are used to evaluate performances: strict, lenient binary tree and lenient sub-expression. The strict evaluation verifies that all bracketed groups of the gold-standard expression are exactly the same as those found in the evaluated expression, providing a score of 1 or 0. The two lenient evaluations compute the ratio between the number of matching groups from a gold expression with those found in the evaluated expression. In other words, lenient is the recall score based on the gold elements.

In lenient binary tree, each fully bracketed expression is parsed as a binary tree. From that tree, each modifier/head pair becomes a basic evaluation element. For example, in *(A (B C))*, two elements *A-C* and *B-C* are used for the evaluation process. This method boosts the performance level on most expressions, but especially those composed of three words, for which a minimum 50% is always obtained.

In lenient sub-expression, evaluation elements are rather sub-expressions to provide a more balanced score. The method extracts each bracketed group except the top-level group and removes all internal parentheses from each one. Thus, from the expression *(((A B) C) D)*, the method extracts *(A B)* and *(A B C)*. The two resulting sub-expressions become gold elements for comparison with those obtained from the evaluated expression. Table 1 shows five examples illustrating score variations using the different methods on expressions of different length.

7 Results

In section 5, we described various approaches to capture, using Wikipedia, the different types of association proposed in our model: lexical, relational and coordinate. We also presented two solutions for combining this more complex model with the bracketing algorithm of section 4 which expects a single type of association, that of dependency. Below, using a dataset of 4749 compound nouns, presented in section 3, we report on some interesting results.

Resource	Algorithm	Strict	Lenient
Wikipedia	Dice	55.00%	67.63%
	PMI	56.25%	68.98%
Google Web Ngram	Dice	51.80%	63.90%
	PMI	60.41%	72.47%

Table 2: Comparing basic association scores in Wikipedia and Google Web.

7.1 Baseline

To measure the impact of combining different types of associations, we first establish our baseline as the bracketing results obtained solely with the basic dependency association scores, as measured on Wikipedia. To further validate our baseline, we wish to compare it to the literature. The closest research providing comparable results on large compounds are Vadas and Curran (2007b) and Pitler et al. (2010), although both focus on supervised approaches, and furthermore, Vadas and Curran (2007b) use contextual features, assuming the noun compounds are to be bracketed in context. Still, Vadas and Curran (2007b) give some baseline results for an unsupervised approach (the supervised approach was promoted in their article) to which we compare our baseline. Far from an ideal comparison (which would be with the exact same dataset and setting), it still provides some indication of the performance of our baseline. They report exact match for complex NPs to be 54.66% for default right branching, 32.66% chi-square dependency and 35.86% chi-square adjacency. As we obtain around 55% for strict matches (see Table 2, first row), we seem above the unsupervised approach they used, which combined their association scores within an implementation of Barker's algorithm.

To confirm that merged Wikipedia pages form a large enough corpus in comparison to most recent work on noun bracketing using web counts (see section 2), we use the English Google Web Ngrams (Lin et al., 2010) (GWN), a 1T corpus contains n-gram counts collected from 1 trillion words of web text, and performed our bracketing algorithm with Wikipedia basic dependency scores, and GWN bigram scores. As shown in Table 2, results are comparable, slightly higher for Dice (55.0% compared to 51.8%) and slightly lower for PMI (56.25% compared to 60.41%).

Throughout our experiments, we have continued using both association measures (Dice and PMI), as well as performing both Barker's algorithm and our bracketing algorithm, but since our algorithm with Dice always gave better results (contrarily to the baseline in which PMI performed better), we only present those results in the following sections.

7.2 Corpus-based improvements

In Section 5, we described how the use of stop words (conjunctions, prepositions, determiners) combined with word pairs of interest could respectively modulate the basic dependency association scores to emphasize coordinate, relational, or lexical association.

For lexical association, word pairs preceded by determiners were searched for in the corpus. We tried different ways of combining association scores between the form with the determiner ("the N1 N2") and the word pair only (N1 N2), such as adding scores, keeping the maximum or minimum score. As well, we tried different ways of combining the scores obtained with the different determiners (a, the, an), again adding, keeping the maximum or the minimum score. Unfortunately, none of these variations helped. We also experimented with searching for plural forms in corpus to emphasize lexical association, which provided a small increase to the baseline as shown in Table 3.

For relational association, we searched for noun pairs with prepositions. The same merging strategies given above for the use of determiners we tried. The best configuration uses a relational boosting strategy of adding scores and a preposition merging strategy of using the minimum score among all prepositions. Even with the best combination, overall, the improvement is marginal as shown in Table 3.

For coordinate association, we searched for noun pairs with conjunctions. Similarly to determiners and prepositions, we tried different merging strategies. Since we are interested in an attenuation of the dependency score with the coordinate score, our merging strategies were of subtracting scores or using

Option	Strict	Lenient	Binary
Baseline	0.5500	0.6763	0.8132
Only including lexical association	0.5842	0.7106	0.8321
Only including relational association	0.5854	0.7093	0.8314
Only including coordinate association	0.5867	0.7110	0.8325

Table 3: Impact of corpus-based statistics (lexical, relational, coordinate association)

Option	Strict	Lenient	Binary
Baseline	0.5500	0.6763	0.8132
Using entity-based refinement (uniform distribution)	0.6020	0.7257	0.8408
Using entity-based compound segmentation	**0.7316**	**0.8213**	**0.8940**

Table 4: Use of entities

the minimum. Again, unfortunately, improvement is marginal, as shown in Table 3.

7.3 Entity-based improvements

Our second approach to promote the lexical unit association score is to find which sub-expressions of the compound are Wikipedia page titles. In Section 5, we suggested two strategies of using these entries, either **score modulation** or *compound segmentation*.

In score modulation, we tried uniform boosting and right boosting as explained in Section 5, with different boosting factors arbitrarily set between 10 and 100. The best result, obtained using a uniform boost with a factor of 50 is presented in Table 4. There is a small improvement using this method. The second strategy of compound segmentation is the one providing the most significant gain. An increase of 13% is obtained for the strict evaluation as shown in the last row of Table 4. For the sake of completeness, we reran all the different variations and parameters which are used for performing the within and between lexical units bracketing. The best configuration required that (1) basic dependency scores were actually replaced by scores obtained by finding plural forms in the corpus (lexical association), (2) determiners were not used, (3) the negative modulation from conjunctions (coordinate association) is obtained by subtracting their frequency from the basic scores, (4) the positive modulation of prepositions (relational association) is obtained by adding their frequency to the basic scores, (5) as different prepositions are searched in corpus, the one with minimum frequency should be taken to alter basic scores, same for conjunctions (6) the head of lexical units is used to measure the "between units" association scores.

7.4 Result analysis

We first note some aspects of the gold standard that would affect the adequacy of our algorithm, and our results.

- ***Noun compound status***: A few examples in the dataset contain very generic adjectives, such as: *(certain ((natural resource) assets))*, *(such ((gas management) contracts))*,*(most (structural engineers))*, or *((too much) attention)*. These are not problematic in themselves, but our statistical approximations for lexical, relational and coordinate associations are not adequate for these cases.

- ***Abbreviations***: Some examples in the gold standard contain abbreviations, for example, *(republican (u.s. sen.))*, *((american president) cos.)* or *(((el dorado) investment) co.)*. Again, these are not problematic in themselves, but we have not yet implemented anything in our algorithm to manage such cases.

- ***Ambiguity***: Some examples found in the gold standard, such as *((sun ((life assurance) society)) plc)* or *((magnetic (resonance imaging)) equipment)* are not obvious to us as being correct.

- ***Compositional examples***: On the positive side, the dataset certainly contains many interesting examples, such as *((new england) ((medical center) hospitals))*, *((northern california) (home prices))*, *(world-wide ((advanced materials) operations))*, *(((lone star) spokesman) (michael london))*, or *((magnetic (resonance imaging)) equipment)*. These examples are interesting because they show a variety of right and left bracketing needed and a variety of named entities and terms of different compositional nature. Research on compound bracketing is required for those examples, as they will probably never end-up in even the most extensive lists of terms and named entities.

To better understand this dataset and the adequacy of our algorithm to its content, we intend, in future work, to perform a manual sampling to determine the types of compounds, and the possible ambiguities.

As for Wikipedia as a resource, it is very valuable and contains many named entities (places, corporations, persons, etc), but it can never contain all entities. For example, we will find *tadeusz mazowiecki* to help in bracketing *(polish (prime minister)) (tadeusz mazowiecki)*, but we will not find *bruno lucisano*, and wrongly bracket *(((rome (film producer)) bruno) lucisano)*.

Independently of the gold standard and the resource used, our method has multiple limitations and peculiarities. We believe that the general approach presented in this research is quite valid: a proposal for the refinement of generic association scores into three subtypes of associations: lexical, relational and coordinate associations. Nevertheless, the statistical approximations used for evaluating the different association types should be revisited and refined.

8 Conclusion

Although bracketing of three-word expressions has been performed quite successfully using unsupervised approaches with web-corpus resources ((Nakov and Hearst, 2005), (Vadas and Curran, 2007b)), compound bracketing of large expressions remains a challenge.

One research direction, taken by Vadas and Curran (2007b) and Pitler et al. (2010) is to investigate supervised learning approaches which will be able to build on the redundancy within the dataset. We take a different direction, that of developing a more complex association model and exploring Wikipedia in an unsupervised manner. Our research presents a noun compound bracketing algorithm which goes beyond the adjacency / dependency models presented so far in the literature. We suggest a method that takes into account different meaning of the proximity of two words, that of being part of the same lexical unit, or being coordinates, or being in a relation.

Our current implementation of our association model certainly provides improvement on the basic association scores, but it does not give a clear view of whether our corpus-based approximations are correct or not. This deserves future investigation into how to best approximate with statistical measures the notions of relational, coordinate and lexical associations. On the other hand, the use of Wikipedia as an encyclopedic resource to help determine lexical units certainly provides the most gain and the best results. On the dataset of 4749 compounds, our best results are 73.16% strict, 82.13% lenient and 89.40% binary tree evaluation. Further use of the structure of Wikipedia can be investigated to help characterize the different types of associations.

An important future goal is to refine the association model, and better anchor it in both linguistic and computational linguistic traditions of noun compound analysis. The model deserves to be studied in its own, regardless of its implementation, which here was performed using Wikipedia. A better understanding of the model and its impact on noun compound bracketing might direct us to better choices for the implementation of the association measures.

Lastly, similarly to other researchers who look at noun compound bracketing as the first step of semantic analysis of NPs to elicit semantic relations (purpose, cause, location, etc) between subgroups of words (Girju et al. (2005), Nastase et al. (2013)), we want to pursue our work into a more fine-grained understanding of noun compounds (Nakov, 2013), combining bracketing with the identification of specific noun relations.

9 Acknowledgements

This research project is partly funded by an NSERC grant RDCPJ417968-11, titled Toward a second generation of an automatic product coding system.

References

Ken Barker. 1998. A Trainable Bracketer for Noun Modifiers. In *Twelfth Canadian Conference on Artificial Intelligence (LNAI 1418).*

Roxana Girju, Dan Moldovan, Marta Tatu, and Daniel Antohe. 2005. On the semantics of noun compounds. *Computer Speech & Language*, 19(4):479–496, October.

Mirella Lapata, Portobello St, S Sheffield, and Frank Keller. 2004. The Web as a Baseline : Evaluating the Performance of Unsupervised Web-based Models for a Range of NLP Tasks. In *Proceedings of the HLT-NAACL*, pages 121–128.

Mark Lauer. 1995. Corpus statistics meet the noun compound: some empirical results. *Proceedings of the 33rd annual meeting on Association for Computational Linguistics*, pages 47–54.

Judith Levi. 1978. *The syntax and semantics of complex nominals.*

D Lin, KW Church, H Ji, and S Sekine. 2010. New Tools for Web-Scale N-grams. *LREC.*

Mitchell P Marcus, Santorini Beatrice, and Mary A Marcinkiewicz. 1994. Building a large annotated corpus of English: the Penn Treebank. *Computational Linguistics*, 19:313–330.

Pierre André Ménard and Caroline Barrière. 2014. Linked Open Data and Web Corpus Data for noun compound bracketing. In *Proceedings of the Ninth International Conference on Language Resources and Evaluation (LREC'14)*, pages 702–709, Reykjavik, Iceland.

Preslav Nakov and M Hearst. 2005. Search engine statistics beyond the n-gram: Application to noun compound bracketing. *Proceedings of the Ninth Conference on Computational Natural Language Learning*, (June):17–24.

Preslav Nakov. 2013. On the interpretation of noun compounds: Syntax, semantics, and entailment. *Natural Language Engineering*, 19(03):291–330, May.

Vivi Nastase, Preslav Nakov, Diarmuid O Seaghdha, and Stan Szpakowicz. 2013. *Semantic Relations Between Nominals.* Morgan and Claypool Publishers.

Emily Pitler, Shane Bergsma, Dekang Lin, and Kenneth Church. 2010. Using web-scale N-grams to improve base NP parsing performance. *Proceedings of the 23rd International Conference on Computational Linguistics*, (August):886–894.

David Vadas and JR Curran. 2007a. Adding noun phrase structure to the Penn Treebank. *45th Annual Meeting of the Association of Computational Linguistics*, (June):240–247.

David Vadas and JR Curran. 2007b. Large-scale supervised models for noun phrase bracketing. *10th Conference of the Pacific Association for Computational Linguistics*, (2004):104–112.

Ralph Weischedel and Ada Brunstein. 2005. BBN pronoun coreference and entity type corpus. Technical report, Linguistic Data Consortium.

Distinguishing Degrees of Compositionality in Compound Splitting for Statistical Machine Translation

Marion Weller[1,2], Fabienne Cap[2], Stefan Müller[1]
Sabine Schulte im Walde[1], Alexander Fraser[2]
[1] IMS, University of Stuttgart
{wellermn;muellesn;schulte}@ims.uni-stuttgart.de
[2] CIS, Ludwig-Maximilian University of Munich
{cap;fraser}@cis.uni-muenchen.de

Abstract

The paper presents an approach to morphological compound splitting that takes the degree of compositionality into account. We apply our approach to German noun compounds and particle verbs within a German–English SMT system, and study the effect of *only splitting compositional compounds* as opposed to an aggressive splitting. A qualitative study explores the translational behaviour of non-compositional compounds.

1 Introduction

In German, as in many other languages, two (or more) simplex words can be combined to form a compound. This is a productive process, leading to a potentially infinite number of sound German compounds. As a consequence, many NLP applications suffer from coverage issues for compounds which do not appear or appear only infrequently in language resources. However, while many compounds are not covered, their component words are often found in lexical resources or training data. Compound processing allows access to these component words and thus can overcome these sparsity issues.

We use Statistical Machine Translation (SMT) as an example application for compound processing. Our SMT system translates from German to English, where compounds are usually split in the German source language prior to training and decoding. The benefits are obvious: vocabulary size is reduced and the languages are adjusted in terms of granularity, as exemplified by the compound *Holzzaun*. This results in better alignment quality and model estimation. Compound splitting also enables the translation of compounds not occurring in the parallel data, if the parts have been seen and can thus be translated individually. However, these assumptions only hold for *compositional* compounds like *Holzzaun* ('wooden fence'), whose meanings can be derived from the meanings of their constituents, namely *Holz* ('wood') and *Zaun* ('fence'). In contrast, the splitting of *non-compositional* compounds may lead to translation errors: e.g. the meaning of *Jägerzaun* ('lattice fence') cannot be represented by the meanings of its constituents *Jäger* ('hunter') and *Zaun* ('fence'). Here, an erroneous splitting of the compound can lead to wrong generalizations or translation pairs, such as *Jäger → lattice*, in the absence of other evidence about how to translate *Jäger*. When splitting compounds for SMT, two important factors should thus be considered: (1) *whether* a compound is compositional and should be split, and if so (2) *how* the compound should be split. Most previous approaches mainly focused on the second task, *how* to split a compound, e.g. using frequency statistics (Koehn and Knight, 2003) or a rule-based morphology (Fritzinger and Fraser, 2010), and all of them showed improved SMT quality for compound splitting. The decision about *whether* the compound is compositional and should be split at all has not received much attention in the past.

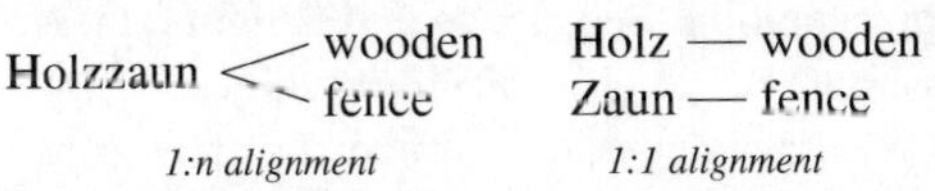

In this work, we examine the effect of *only splitting compositional compounds*, in contrast to splitting all compounds. To this end, we combine (A) an approach relying on the distributional similarity between compounds and their constituents, to predict the degree of compositionality and thus to determine *whether* to split the compound with (B) a combination of morphological and frequency-based features

Proceedings of the First Workshop on Computational Approaches to Compound Analysis, pages 81–90,
Dublin, Ireland, August 24 2014.

to determine *how* to split a compound. We experiment with this novel semantically-informed compound splitting on the source-side data of a German-English SMT system. As far as we know, we are the first to study the impact of compositionality-aware compound splitting in SMT. We evaluate our systems on a standard and on a specifically created test set, both for noun compounds and particle verbs. Our results show that phrase-based SMT is generally robust with regard to over-splitting non-compositional compounds, with the exception of low-frequency words. This is in line with corresponding assumptions from previous work. Furthermore, we present a small-scale study about the translational behaviour of non-compositional compounds, which can surprisingly often be translated component-wise.

2 Related Work

We combine morphology-based compound splitting with distributional semantics to improve phrase-based SMT. Here, we discuss relevant work of compound splitting in SMT and distributional semantics.

2.1 Compound Splitting in SMT

Compound splitting in SMT is a well-studied task. There is a wide range of previous work, including purely string- and frequency-based approaches, but also linguistically-informed approaches. All lines of research improved translation performance due to compound splitting. In Koehn and Knight (2003), compounds are split through the identification of substrings from a corpus. The splitting is performed without linguistic knowledge (except for the insertion of the filler letters "(e)s"), which necessarily leads to many erroneous splittings. Multiple possible splitting options are disambiguated using the frequencies of the substrings. Starting from Koehn and Knight (2003), Stymne (2008) covers more morphological transformations and imposes POS constraints on the subwords. Nießen and Ney (2000) and Fritzinger and Fraser (2010) perform compound splitting by relying on morphological analysers to identify suitable split points. This has the advantage of returning only linguistically motivated splitting options, but the analyses are often ambiguous and require disambiguation: Nießen and Ney (2000) use a parser for context-sensitive disambiguation, and Fritzinger and Fraser (2010) use corpus frequencies to find the best split for each compound. Other approaches use a two-step word alignment process: first, word alignment is performed on a split representation of the compounding language. Then, all former compound parts for which there is no aligned counterpart in the non-compounding language are merged back to the compound again. Finally, word alignment is re-run on this representation. See Koehn and Knight (2003) for experiments on German, DeNeefe et al. (2008) for Arabic and Bai et al. (2008) for Chinese. This blocks non-compositional compounds from being split if they are translated as one simplex English word in the training data (e.g. *Heckenschütze*, lit. 'hedge|shooter'; 'sniper') and aligned correctly. However, cases like *Jägerzaun*, 'lattice fence' are not covered.

In the present work, we identify compounds with a morphological analyser, disambiguated with corpus frequencies. Moreover, we restrict splitting to compositional compounds using distributional semantics. We are not aware of any previous work that takes semantics into account for compound splitting in SMT.

2.2 Distributional Semantics and Compounding

Distributional information has been a steadily increasing, integral part of lexical semantic research over the past 20 years. Based on the *distributional hypothesis* (Firth, 1957; Harris, 1968) that "you shall know a word by the company it keeps", distributional semantics exploits the co-occurrence of words in corpora to explore the meanings and the similarities of the words, phrases, sentences, etc. of interest.

Among many other tasks, distributional semantic information has been utilised to determine the degree of compositionality (or: semantic transparency) of various types of compounds, most notably regarding noun compounds (e.g., Zinsmeister and Heid (2004), Reddy et al. (2011), Schulte im Walde et al. (2013), Salehi et al. (2014)) and particle verbs (e.g., McCarthy et al. (2003), Bannard (2005), Cook and Stevenson (2006), Kühner and Schulte im Walde (2010), Bott and Schulte im Walde (2014), Salehi et al. (2014)). Typically, these approaches rely on co-occurrence information from a corpus (either referring to bags-of-words, or focusing on target-specific types of features), and compare the distributional features of the compounds with those of the constituents, in order to predict the degree of compositionality of the

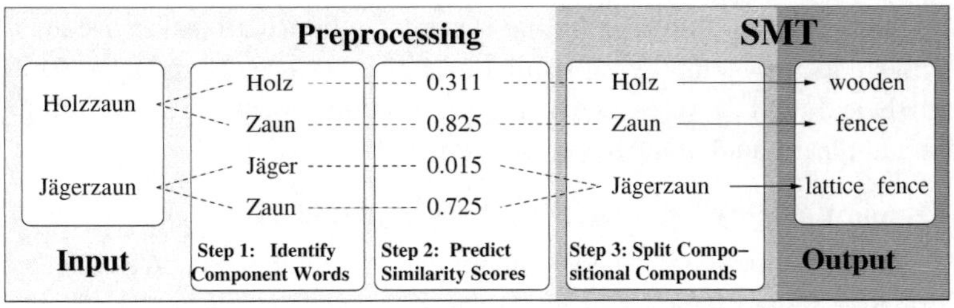

Figure 1: Semantically-informed compound processing in SMT.

compound. The underlying assumption is that a compound which is similar in meaning to a constituent (as in *Holzzaun–Zaun* ('wooden fence'–'fence') but not in *Löwenzahn–Zahn* ('lion|tooth (dandelion)'–'tooth')) is also similar to the constituent with regard to co-occurrence information.

Most related to this work on noun compounds, Reddy et al. (2011) relied on window-based distributional models to predict the compositionality of English noun compounds, and Schulte im Walde et al. (2013) compared window-based against syntax-based distributional models to predict the compositionality of German noun compounds. Zinsmeister and Heid (2004) used subcategorising verbs to predict compound–head similarities of German noun compounds. Most recently, Salehi et al. (2014) extended the previous approaches to take multi-lingual co-occurrence information into account, regarding English and German noun compounds, and English particle verbs.

3 Methodology

We integrate our semantically-informed compound splitting as a pre-processing step to the German source language of an SMT system. See Figure 1 for an illustration of our compound processing pipeline.

3.1 Target Compounds

German compounds are combinations of two (or more) simplex words. In some cases, a morphological transformation is required: for example, when combining the two nouns *Ausflug* ('excursion') and *Ziel* ('destination') → *Ausflugsziel* ('excursion destination'), a filler letter (here: *"s"*) needs to be inserted. Other such transformations include more filler letters or the deletion/substitution of letters.
Noun compounds are formed of a head noun and a modifier, which can consist of nouns, verbs, adjectives or proper nouns.
Particle verbs are productive compositions of a base verb and a prefix particle, whose part-of-speech varies between open-class nouns, adjectives, and verbs, and closed-class prepositions and adverbs. In comparison to noun compounds, the constituents of German particle verbs exhibit a much higher degree of ambiguity: Verbs in general are more ambiguous than nouns, and the largest sub-class of particles (those with a preposition particle) is highly ambiguous by itself (e.g. Lechler and Roßdeutscher (2009) and Springorum (2011)). For example, in *anknabbern* ('to nibble partially'), the particle *an* expresses a partitive meaning , whereas in *ankleben* ('to glue onto sth.') *an* has a topological meaning (*to glue sth. onto an implicit background*). In addition, particle verb senses may be transparent or opaque with respect to their base verbs. For example, *abholen* 'fetch' is rather transparent with respect to its base verb *holen* 'fetch', whereas *anfangen* 'begin' is more opaque with respect to *fangen* 'catch'. In contrast, *einsetzen* has both transparent (e.g. 'insert') and opaque (e.g. 'begin') verb senses with respect to *setzen* 'put/sit (down)'. The high degree of ambiguity makes particle verbs a challenge for NLP. Moreover, particle and base verb can occur separately (*er fängt an*: 'he begins') or in one word (*dass er anfängt*: 'that he begins'), depending on the clausal type. This makes consistent treatment of particle verbs difficult.

3.2 Identification of Component Parts

We use the rule-based morphological analyser SMOR (Schmid et al., 2004) to identify compounds and their constituents in our parallel training data (cf. Section 4). It relies on a large lexicon of word lemmas and feature rules for productive morphological processes in German, i.e., compounding, derivation and inflection. In this paper, we will not consider splitting into derivational affixes (as needed for, e.g., Arabic and Turkish), but instead identify simplex words that may also occur independently. Moreover, we only keep noun compounds and particle verbs consisting of two constituents. The resulting set consists of 93,299 noun compound types and 3,689 particle verb types.

3.3 Predicting Compositionality based on Distributional Similarity

Starting from this set of compounds as derived from our parallel training data, we collected distributional co-occurrence information from two large German web corpora and the machine translation training data: (i) the German *COW* corpus (Schäfer and Bildhauer (2012), ~9 billion words), (ii) the *SdeWaC* (Faaß and Eckart (2013), ~880 million words), (iii) our MT parallel corpus (~40 million words) and (iv) MT language model training data (~146 million words). We relied on earlier work and used the 20,000 most frequent nouns from the SdeWaC as co-occurrence features, looking into a window of 20 words to the left and to the right of our target compounds and their constituents. We thus obtained a co-occurrence matrix of all compounds and their constituents with the 20,000 selected nouns. As co-occurrence strength (i.e., how strong is a co-occurrence between a target word and a co-occurring noun), we collected frequencies and transformed them into *local mutual information (LMI)* values, cf. Evert (2005). Finally, we calculated the distributional similarity between the compounds and their constituents, relying on the standard measure *cosine*. The cosine value is then used to predict the degree of compositionality between the respective compound–constituent pairs. For example, the cosine value of the pair *Baumschule–Baum*[1] is 0.38, while the cosine value of the pair *Baumschule–Schule* is only 0.01.

3.4 Semantically-Informed Compound Splitting

In the two preceding sections, we described how we identified component words and calculated distributional compositionality scores for all of the compounds found in our training data. Here, we give details on how we include the semantic information into the compound splitting process. Recall that we only want to split compositional compounds and keep non-compositional compounds together.

The splitting decision (to split/not split a compound) is based on the compositionality score of the compound that takes into account either one or both of the compound–constituent cosine values: if the predicted degree of compositionality is high, the compound is split. We consider and combine four different criteria: i) only the compound–modifier similarity (*mod*); (ii) only the compound–head similarity (*head*); a combination of the compound–modifier and the compound–head similarities, relying on (iii) the geometric mean (*geom*) or (iv) on the arithmetic mean (*arith*). We used different thresholds for each of these criteria throughout our experiments, with a specific focus on distinguishing the contributions of the modifiers vs. the heads in the splitting decision, following insights from recent work in psycholinguistic studies (Gagné and Spalding, 2009; Gagné and Spalding, 2011) as well as in computational approaches on noun compounding (Reddy et al., 2011; Schulte im Walde et al., 2013). Furthermore, we compare the effects of splitting with regard to two types of compounds, noun compounds and particle verbs: Both types are very productive and can generate a potentially infinite number of new forms.

4 Experimental Setting

This section gives an overview on the technical details of the SMT system and our data sets. Compound splitting is applied to all source-language data, i.e. the parallel data used to train the model, as well as the input for parameter tuning and testing.[2]

Translation Model Moses is a state-of-the-art toolkit for phrase-based SMT systems (Koehn et al., 2007). We use it with default settings to train a translation model and we do so separately for each of the different compound splittings. Word alignment is performed using GIZA++ (Och and Ney, 2003). Feature weights are tuned using Batch-Mira (Cherry and Foster, 2012) with *'-safe-hope'* until convergence.

Training Data Our parallel training data contains the Europarl corpus (version 4, cf. Koehn (2005)) and also newspaper texts, overall ca. 1.5 million sentences[3] (roughly 44 million words). In addition, we

[1] *Baum|schule*: 'tree|school' (tree nursery)

[2] Compounds not contained in the parallel data are always split, as they cannot be translated otherwise.

[3] Data from the shared task of the EACL 2009 workshop on statistical machine translation: `www.statmt.org/wmt09`

use an English corpus of roughly 227 million words (including the English part of the parallel data) to build a target-side 5-gram language model with SRILM (Stolcke, 2002) in combination with KENLM (Heafield, 2011). For parameter tuning, we use 1,025 sentences of news data.

Standard Test set 1,026 sentences of news data (test set from the 2009 WMT Shared Task): this set is to measure the translation quality on a standard SMT test and make it comparable to other work.

Noun/Verb Test set As our main focus lies on sentences containing compounds, we created a second test set which is rich in compounds. From the combined 2008-2013 Shared Task test sets, we extracted all sentences containing at least one noun compound for which we have compound-constituent similarity scores. Moreover, we excluded sentences containing nouns that are not in the parallel training data: such compounds can only be translated when split which allows to translate their components. The final test set consists of 2,574 sentences. Similarly, we also created a set rich in particle verbs (855 sentences).

Opaque Test set As the two first test sets mainly contain compositional compounds, we use a third test set consisting of sentences with only non-compositional compounds. The underlying compounds were chosen based on a list containing noun compounds and human ratings for compositionality (von der Heide and Borgwaldt (2009)). As before, the compounds must have occurred in the parallel data. The result is a list of 14 compounds, of which 11 have a low modifier-compound similarity and 3 have a low head-compound similarity. We then extracted sentences containing these compounds (5 per compound = 70 in total) from German newspaper data[4]. In contrast to the other sets, we use this test set in a qualitative study, to approximate the translation quality by counting the number of correctly translated compounds.

5 SMT Results

In this section, we present and discuss the results of our machine translation experiments. We first report results for two test sets in terms of a standard evaluation metric (BLEU) and then continue with a small-scale qualitative study on the translational behaviour of non-compositional compounds.

5.1 Compound Splitting within a Standard SMT Task

BLEU (Papineni et al., 2002) is a common metric to automatically measure the quality of SMT output by comparing n gram matches of the SMT output with a human reference translation. Table 1 lists the results for our SMT-systems: we report on different compound-constituent scores and thresholds, for noun compounds and particle verbs respectively. Note that BLEU scores are not comparable across different test sets, but only illustrate system differences within one test set. We compare our systems to the scores of a *baseline system* (without compound processing) and an *aggressive split* system in which all noun compounds and particle verbs are split. The labels *DIST* and *FREQ* indicate how several possible splittings were disambiguated: *DIST* means we chose the splitting option having the higher geometric mean of the two compound-constituent scores, assuming that the variant expressing a higher compositionality score leads to the more probable splitting analysis. For *FREQ*, the decision is based on the geometric mean of corpus frequencies of the respective components of the compound, as is common practise for the disambiguation of multiple splitting options in SMT (Koehn and Knight, 2003; Fritzinger and Fraser, 2010). In terms of BLEU, there is little difference for these two variants. For further experiments, we thus decided to always use *FREQ* for disambiguation, assuming that components chosen by frequency are potentially better repre-

		nouns		particle verbs	
		stand.	**noun**	**stand.**	**verb**
baseline		21.00	21.08	21.00	20.29
aggr	DIST	22.00	22.02	21.02	20.11
aggr	FREQ	22.04	21.88	21.11	20.21
0.05	head	21.77	21.58	–	–
0.05	mod.	22.01	21.74	–	–
0.05	geom.	21.99	21.71	–	–
0.05	arith.	21.95	21.95	–	–
0.1	head	21.91	21.69	21.11	20.24
0.1	mod.	22.01	21.63	20.98	20.43
0.1	geom.	22.06	21.90	21.12	20.55
0.1	arith.	22.05	21.73	21.08	20.34
0.15	head	21.80	21.67	21.10	20.09
0.15	mod.	21.71	21.77	21.00	20.25
0.15	geom.	21.78	21.64	20.84	20.30
0.15	arith.	22.00	21.77	21.24	20.40
0.2	head	21.78	21.51	–	–
0.2	mod.	21.78	21.45	–	–
0.2	geom.	21.76	21.54	–	–
0.2	arith.	22.02	21.79	–	–

Table 1: BLEU scores for all compound-constituent variations.

[4] www.ims.uni-stuttgart.de/forschung/ressourcen/korpora/hgc.html

rating	compound	gloss	mod.	head	translation
HIGHLY	Staats|bankrott	nation|bankruptcy	0.4779	0.6527	*national bankruptcy*
COMP.	Staats|gebilde	nation|structure	0.6955	0.3431	*national structure*
MEDIUM	Industrie|staat	industry|nation	0.0258	0.1488	*industrial nation*
COMP.	Staats|kasse	nation|cash box	0.0718	0.2757	*public purse, treasury*
LOW	Staats|spitze	nation|top	0.0024	0.0040	*top/head of state*
COMP.	Staats|monotheismus	nation|monotheism	0.0071	0.0071	*national monotheism*

Table 2: Examples for different compound-constitutent score ranges: HIGH: highly compositional, MEDIUM: cases of doubt, LOW: highly non-compositional, according to their scores.

sented in the training data. Thus, we first use frequencies to determine the best split option in the case of several possibilities, and then we apply distributional semantics to determine whether to split at all. The remainder of Table 1 reports on different variants of the semantically-informed splitting criteria we used. The notation *head/mod/geom/arith* indicates which (combination of) compound-constituent scores were applied as criterion, with the threshold indicated by the vertical number. We performed the first set of experiments with different thresholds for noun compounds, and then applied the medium-range thresholds to the particle verbs. Generally, there are no considerable differences between the systems with semantically restricted splitting and the *aggressive split* systems, even though there seems to be a slightly positive effect for particle verbs. Having a closer look, we find that for noun compounds on the standard test set, the best results (threshold: 0.1) are at the same level as the *aggressive split* systems; with some small losses in BLEU on some of the other settings.

5.2 Discussion

All settings clearly outperform the baseline system (without compound processing). This indicates that phrase-based SMT is rather robust with regard to non-semantic splitting as it is can often recover from over-splitting by translating the word sequence as a phrase. This is in line with previous observations of Koehn and Knight (2003). The results for the noun test set, which is biased towards containing more nominal compounds, even suggests that less splitting might harm the system, as the BLEU scores tend to drop when increasing the threshold. For particle verbs,[5] the picture is slightly different: first, splitting only particle verbs does not lead to a considerable improvement over the baseline, as in the case of noun compounds. For the verb test set, it even leads to a drop in BLEU. However, a more restricted splitting leads to improved BLEU scores, even though not significantly better than the un-split baseline system. Even though the handling of particle verbs needs to be refined in terms of dealing with their structural behaviour (split vs. unsplit depending on the sentence structure) or ambiguities of the particle verb, we consider this an encouraging result indicating that particle verbs can benefit from a semantically-informed splitting process.

There are several possible reasons why a more restricted splitting might not lead to an improvement, even though the idea of splitting only compositional compounds is intuitive and straightforward.

Inconsistent Splitting Compositionality is a continuum rather than a binary decision, with the scores of many (compositional) compounds being in the medium range. Thus, it happens that some compounds containing a certain constituent are split, whereas others are not: such inconsistent splittings do not contribute to the generalization compound splitting aims for. Table 2 gives examples for compounds with different degrees of compositionality, which illustrate this issue: for *Industriestaat* ('industrial nation') and *Staatskasse* ('public purse') in the middle part of the table, a splitting decision based on the *head* scores for thresholds of 0.15 or 0.2 leads to inconsistent splitting. Only compounds with high scores, as the examples at the top of Table 2 are always split. The bottom part gives examples with comparatively low compound-constituent scores that would benefit from splitting, but which will not be split in any of our systems.

[5]Note that there are considerably less particle verbs than noun compounds in the standard test set and the parallel data.

compound	gloss	translation	unsplit	f	split	f
Seehunde	*sea|dogs*	*seals*	seals	5	seals	5
Flohmarkt	*flea|market*	*flea market*	flea market	5	flea market	5
Kopfsalat	*head|salad*	*lettuce*	lettuce	5	lettuce	5
Handtuch	*hand|cloth*	*towel*	towel	5	towel	5
Kronleuchter	*crown|candelabra*	*chandelier*	chandelier	5	crown leuchter	5
Gürteltiere	*belt|animal*	*armadillo*	armadillos	5	belt animals	5
Wasserhahn	*water|rooster*	*tap*	tap	5	water tap water supply	2 3
Meerschweinchen	*sea|piglet*	*guinea pig*	guinea pig	5	guinea pig sea pig	4 1
Taschenbuch	*pocket|book*	*paperback*	paperback	5	paper back pocket book	3 2
Kronkorken	*crown|cork*	*crown cap*	*kronkorken	5	crown corks	5
Taschenlampe	*pocket|lamp*	*flashlight*	*taschenlampe	5	pocket lamp bag lamp	4 1
Fleischwolf	*meat|wolf*	*meat grinder*	*fleischwolf	5	meat wolf	5
Marienkäfer	*Mary|bug*	*ladybug*	*marienkäfer	5	*marie käfer	5
Blockflöten	*block|flute*	*recorder*	*blockflöten	5	block might bloc might	4 1

Table 3: correct vs. wrong – Translation of non-compositional compounds (opaque test set) without being split (*unsplit*) vs. being *split* prior to translation. '*' highlights untranslated compounds.

Coverage of Opaque Compounds Another relevant factor concerns the frequency ranges of compounds that are most interesting for this approach. High/mid frequency compounds are usually well-covered by the training data of an SMT system, and in most cases they are translated correctly even if they have been split erroneously. This is due to the fact that split compounds can be learned and translated as a phrase if there were enough instances for the system to learn a valid translation. In the case of low-frequency compounds, the system is less likely to learn a correct translation from the parallel data. However, low-frequency compounds are not well covered by the system and splitting should thus be highly beneficial. Newly created, i.e. highly compositional compounds, tend to be of low frequency, as is illustrated by the example of *Staatsmonotheismus* (freq=1 in the parallel data) in Table 2. However, a wrong splitting decision for a non-compositional compound of low frequency is likely to lead to an incorrect translation as the SMT system has better statistics for the individual parts than for the sequence of the compounds constituents. We assume that for low-frequency compounds the distributional similarity scores are generally less reliable, even though using LMI helps to minimize this. To a certain extent, we expect non-compositional compounds –which are typically considered as lexicalized– to occur with higher frequencies than novel compositional compounds.[6] Furthermore, there are considerably more compositional than non-compositional compounds in standard text. Thus, being in favor of splitting in the case of low-frequency words should be reasonable in most contexts.

6 A Closer Look at Translating Opaque Compounds

In this section, we compare the translations of non-compositional compounds when they are unsplit and when they are split. We use a small test set containing 70 sentences, 5 for each of the 14 non-compositional compounds (see Section 4). Then we conduct a small-scale qualitative analysis focusing on the correct translation of opaque compounds.

Table 3 reports on correct translations for the non-compositional compounds for an experiment where they have been *split* or not split (*unsplit*) prior to translation. Even though all compounds occurred in the parallel data, five (which are marked with '*') cannot be translated by the unsplit system due to not being aligned correctly. The other compounds are translated correctly (marked with "+" in Table 3). In the course of our study, we found that many of the correct translations remain the same (*seals, flea market, lettuce, towel*). In the case of *guinea pig, paperback* and *tap* there are mixed results of correct and incorrect translations. Only in the cases of *chandelier* ("*crown leuchter*") and *armadillo* ("*belt animal*"),

[6] It has to be noted, though, that the model is influenced by the somewhat different domain of the parallel data (European Parliament proceedings, a standard data set for SMT).

compound	gloss	translation
Bärlauch	*bear|leek*	*bear leek*
Baumschule	*tree|school*	*tree nursery*
Löwenanteil	*lion|share*	*lion's share*
Fliegenpilz	*fly|mushroom*	*fly agaric*
Flohmarkt	*flea|market*	*flea market*

compound	gloss	translation
Handtasche	*hand|bag*	*handbag*
Hirschkäfer	*stag|beetle*	*stag beetle*
Hüttenkäse	*cottage|cheese*	*cottage cheese*
Kronkorken	*crown|cork*	*crown cap*
Teelicht	*tea|light*	*tea candle*

Table 4: Examples for (near) literal translation of non-compositional compounds.

which were translated correctly with the *unsplit* system, all translations obtained with the *split* system are wrong. Somewhat surprisingly, in some cases there even is a benefit from splitting the non-compositional compounds: *Kronkorken*, previously not translated at all, is correctly generated as *crown cork*. For other previously untranslated words, *Fleischwolf* and *Taschenlampe*, literal translations of the constituents are given: while *meat wolf* (instead of *meat grinder*) is probably not understandable, the translation of *Taschenlampe* as *pocket lamp* is certainly preferable to the untranslated compound.

Due to the observed unexpected translational behaviour of 2 of the 14 non-compositional compounds (*Flohmarkt* and *Kronkorken*), which can be translated literally and thus –in theory– benefit from splitting, we present a small study illustrating that this phenomenon is not as rare as one would intuitively expect. This study is not meant to be comprehensive, but rather to point out that the translational behaviour of non-compositional compounds can correspond to that of compositional compounds; Table 4 lists a few such examples. We assume that this behaviour is due to the fact that English and German are similar languages with a similar background. Thus, the "images" used in non-compositional words often tend to be similar. For some of the compounds (e.g. *Flohmarkt*) this is even true for some Romance languages, too (IT: *mercato delle pulci*, FR: *marché aux puces*) .

Generally, the SMT system should even be able to handle cases where the translation of one part is not strictly literal (e.g. *cap–cork* or *agaric–mushroom*). In comparison to a dictionary, which only lists few translations, the translation model offers a large choice of translation options that are not always strictly synonymous, but can cover a large range of related meanings. In combination with the target-side language model, this could allow to "guess" good translations of such compounds. However, the component-wise translation of non-compositional compounds only works if the source- and target language compounds contain the same number of constituents. For example, consider translating the word *Faultier* (*lazy|animal*: "*sloth*"): even if the SMT system offers the translation *faul–sloth*, it would also need to produce a translation for the constituent *tier*, probably resulting in something like *sloth animal*.

In conclusion, while phrase-based SMT is often able to recover from over-splitting by translating a word sequence as a phrase, this is not always necessary for opaque compounds as they can have a literal or near-literal translation. Thus, for explicitly handling non-compositional compounds in SMT, a monolingual estimation of compositionality is not the only relevant factor. The translational behaviour of compounds should also be taken into account.

7 Conclusion and Future Work

We studied the impact of compositionality in German-English SMT by restricting compound splitting to compositional compounds. The decision about compositionality is based on the distributional similarity between a compound and its constituents. We experimented with different threshold/score combinations on a standard and a specifically created test set. Our results indicate that phrase-based SMT is very robust with regard to over-splitting non-compositional noun compounds, with the exception of low-frequency compounds. Furthermore, we studied the translational behaviour of non-compositional compounds with a special focus on the fact that non-compositional compounds can in some cases be translated component-wise, leading to the conclusion that a monolingual estimation of compositionality is not sufficient for an optimal explicit handling of compounds in SMT applications.

The relatively low impact of distinguishing the degree of compositionality might also be due to the fact that the task of translating noun compounds can be considered "easy", as the split components always occur adjacently. In contrast, handling other types of non-compositional structures (e.g. noun-verb or preposition-noun-verb combinations which are non-compositional) is a challenging task for future work.

Acknowledgements

This work was funded by the DFG Research Projects "Distributional Approaches to Semantic Relatedness" (Marion Weller, Stefan Müller) and "Models of Morphosyntax for Statistical Machine Translation – Phase 2" (Fabienne Cap, Alexander Fraser, Marion Weller) and the DFG Heisenberg Fellowship SCHU-2580/1-1 (Sabine Schulte im Walde).

References

Ming-Hong Bai, Keh-Jiann Chen, and Jason S Chang. 2008. Improving word alignment by adjusting chinese word segmentation. In *IJCNLP'08: Proceedings of the 3rd International Joint Conference on Natural Language Processing*, pages 249–256.

Collin Bannard. 2005. Learning about the Meaning of Verb–Particle Constructions from Corpora. *Computer Speech and Language*, 19:467–478.

Stefan Bott and Sabine Schulte im Walde. 2014. Optimizing a Distributional Semantic Model for the Prediction of German Particle Verb Compositionality. In *Proceedings of the 9th Conference on Language Resources and Evaluation*, Reykjavik, Iceland.

Colin Cherry and George Foster. 2012. Batch tuning strategies for statistical machine translation. In *HLT-NAACL'12: Proceedings of the Human Language Technology Conference of the North American Chapter of the Association for Computational Linguistics*, volume 12, pages 34–35.

Paul Cook and Suzanne Stevenson. 2006. Classifying Particle Semantics in English Verb-Particle Constructions. In *Proceedings of the ACL/COLING Workshop on Multiword Expressions: Identifying and Exploiting Underlying Properties*, pages 45–53, Sydney, Australia.

Steve DeNeefe, Ulf Hermjakob, and Kevin Knight. 2008. Overcoming vocabulary sparsity in mt using lattices. In *AMTA'08: Proceedings of the 8th Biennial Conference of the Association for Machine Translation in the Americas*.

Stefan Evert. 2005. *The Statistics of Word Co-Occurrences: Word Pairs and Collocations*. Ph.D. thesis, Institut für Maschinelle Sprachverarbeitung, Universität Stuttgart.

Gertrud Faaß and Kerstin Eckart. 2013. SdeWaC – a Corpus of Parsable Sentences from the Web. In *Proceedings of the International Conference of the German Society for Computational Linguistics and Language Technology*, pages 61–68, Darmstadt, Germany.

John R. Firth. 1957. *Papers in Linguistics 1934-51*. Longmans, London, UK.

Fabienne Fritzinger and Alexander Fraser. 2010. How to Avoid Burning Ducks: Combining Linguistic Analysis and Corpus Statistics for German Compound Processing. In *Proceedings of the Fifth Workshop on Statistical Machine Translation*, pages 224–234. Association for Computational Linguistics.

Christina L. Gagné and Thomas L. Spalding. 2009. Constituent Integration during the Processing of Compound Words: Does it involve the Use of Relational Structures? *Journal of Memory and Language*, 60:20–35.

Christina L. Gagné and Thomas L. Spalding. 2011. Inferential Processing and Meta-Knowledge as the Bases for Property Inclusion in Combined Concepts. *Journal of Memory and Language*, 65:176–192.

Zellig Harris. 1968. Distributional Structure. In Jerold J. Katz, editor, *The Philosophy of Linguistics*, Oxford Readings in Philosophy, pages 26–47. Oxford University Press.

Kenneth Heafield. 2011. Kenlm: faster and smaller language model queries. In *EMNLP'11: Proceedings of the 6th workshop on statistical machine translation within the 8th Conference on Empirical Methods in Natural Language Processing*, pages 187–197.

Philipp Koehn and Kevin Knight. 2003. Empirical methods for compound splitting. In *EACL '03. Proceedings of the 10th Conference of the European Chapter of the Association for Computational Linguistics*, pages 187–193, Morristown, NJ, USA. Association for Computational Linguistics.

Philipp Koehn, Hieu Hoang, Alexandra Birch, Chris Callison-Burch, Marcello Federico, Nicola Bertoldi, Brooke Cowan, Wade Shen, Christine Moran, Richard Zens, Chris Dyer, Ondrej Bojar, Alexandra Constantin, and Evan Herbst. 2007. Moses: Open source toolkit for statistical machine translation. In *ACL'07: Proceedings of the 45th Annual Meeting of the Association for Computational Linguistics, Demonstration Session*, pages 177–180.

Philipp Koehn. 2005. Europarl: a parallel corpus for statistical machine translation. In *MT Summit'05: Proceedings of the 10th machine translation summit*, pages 79–86.

Natalie Kühner and Sabine Schulte im Walde. 2010. Determining the Degree of Compositionality of German Particle Verbs by Clustering Approaches. In *Proceedings of the 10th Conference on Natural Language Processing*, pages 47–56, Saarbrücken, Germany.

Andrea Lechler and Antje Roßdeutscher. 2009. German Particle Verbs with *auf*. Reconstructing their Composition in a DRT-based Framework. *Linguistische Berichte*, 220.

Diana McCarthy, Bill Keller, and John Carroll. 2003. Detecting a Continuum of Compositionality in Phrasal Verbs. In *Proceedings of the ACL-SIGLEX Workshop on Multiword Expressions: Analysis, Acquisition and Treatment*, pages 73–80, Sapporo, Japan.

Sonja Nießen and Hermann Ney. 2000. Improving SMT quality with morpho-syntactic analysis. In *COLING'00: Proceedings of the 18th International Conference on Computational Linguistics*, pages 1081–1085. Morgan Kaufmann.

Franz Josef Och and Hermann Ney. 2003. A systematic comparison of various statistical alignment models. *Computational Linguistics*, 29(1):19–51,.

Kishore Papineni, Salim Roukos, Todd Ward, and Wei-Jing Zhu. 2002. Bleu: A method for automatic evaluation of machine translation. In *ACL'02: Proceedings of the 40th Annual Meeting of the Association for Computational Linguistics*, pages 311–318.

Siva Reddy, Diana McCarthy, and Suresh Manandhar. 2011. An Empirical Study on Compositionality in Compound Nouns. In *Proceedings of the 5th International Joint Conference on Natural Language Processing*, pages 210–218, Chiang Mai, Thailand.

Bahar Salehi, Paul Cook, and Timothy Baldwin. 2014. Using Distributional Similarity of Multi-Way Translations to Predict Multiword Expression Compositionality. In *Proceedings of EACL 2014.*

Roland Schäfer and Felix Bildhauer. 2012. Building Large Corpora from the Web Using a New Efficient Tool Chain. In *Proceedings of the 8th International Conference on Language Resources and Evaluation*, pages 486–493, Istanbul, Turkey.

Helmut Schmid, Arne Fitschen, and Ulrich Heid. 2004. Smor: A German computational morphology covering derivation, composition and inflection. In *LREC '04: Proceedings of the 4th Conference on Language Resources and Evaluation*, pages 1263–1266.

Sabine Schulte im Walde, Stefan Müller, and Stephen Roller. 2013. Exploring Vector Space Models to Predict the Compositionality of German Noun-Noun Compounds. In *Proceedings of the 2nd Joint Conference on Lexical and Computational Semantics*, pages 255–265, Atlanta, GA.

Sylvia Springorum. 2011. DRT-based Analysis of the German Verb Particle *"an"*. *Leuvense Bijdragen*, 97:80–105.

Andreas Stolcke. 2002. SRILM – an extensible language modelling toolkit. In *ICSLN'02: Proceedings of the international conference on spoken language processing*, pages 901–904.

Sara Stymne. 2008. German compounds in factored statistical machine translation. In *GoTAL '08: Proceedings of the 6th International Conference on Natural Language Processing*, pages 464–475. Springer Verlag.

Claudia von der Heide and Susanne Borgwaldt. 2009. Assoziationen zu Unter, Basis und Oberbegriffen. In *Proceedings of the 9th Norddeutsches Linguistisches Kolloquium*, pages 51–74.

Heike Zinsmeister and Ulrich Heid. 2004. Collocations of Complex Nouns: Evidence for Lexicalisation. In *Proceedings of Konvens*, Vienna, Austria.

Author Index

Association for Computational Linguistics
209 N. Eighth Street
Stroudsburg, Pennsylvania 18360